REACT
Reflect and Evaluate

Activities for Secondary Religious Education

religious laws and human behavi
human-rights issue
belonging to a religious commun

Rosemary Pratt,
Sylvia and Barry Sutcliffe

RMEP

RELIGIOUS AND MORAL EDUCATION PRESS

Published by Religious and Moral Education Press
A division of SCM-Canterbury Press Ltd
A wholly owned subsidiary of Hymns Ancient & Modern Ltd
St Mary's Works, St Mary's Plain
Norwich, Norfolk NR3 3BH

Copyright © 1999 Rosemary Pratt, Sylvia and Barry Sutcliffe

Rosemary Pratt, Sylvia and Barry Sutcliffe have asserted their right under the Copyright, Designs and Patents Act, 1988, to be identified as Authors of this Work.

All rights reserved. Parts of this book may be photocopied by the purchaser or the purchaser's school/organization for use within that school/organization only. The photocopying of inspection copies is not permitted.

First published 1999

ISBN 1 85175 134 3

Acknowledgements

Extracts reproduced in the book are from the following sources:

What the Buddha Taught, Walpola Rahula (Gordon Fraser, London, 1967): pp.19, 48
Rehat Maryada (Shiromani Gurdwara Parbandhak Committee, Amritsar, 1978): pp.23, 53
'The Joy Hidden in Sorrow: Reflections given by Sister Medhanandi at the Death and Dying Retreat, Amaravati Buddhist Monastery, November 1996' (*Forest Sangha Newsletter* 41, July 1997, p.6): p.69
Scriptures quoted from the *Good News Bible* published by The Bible Societies/HarperCollins Publishers Ltd UK © American Bible Society, 1966, 1971, 1976, 1992: pp.14 (Matt. 6:9–14), 19, 21, 22, 49 (Luke 12:6, 1 Cor. 6:19, Matt. 26:52, 5:9, 5:38–39, 10:34, Rom. 13:1–2), 52 (Deut. 16:18)
Scripture quotations taken from the HOLY BIBLE, NEW INTERNATIONAL VERSION. Copyright © 1973, 1978, 1984 by International Bible Society. Used by permission: pp.14 (Exod. 34: 6–7), 49 (1 Cor. 3: 16–17, Rom. 12:17, Matt. 7:1), 52 (all except Deut. 16:18)
The Bhagavad Gita: A Verse Translation, Geoffrey Parrinder (Sheldon Press, London, 1974): pp.20, 50
The Upanishads, trans. Erknath Easwaran (Arkana/Penguin, New York, 1988): p.13
The Upanishads, trans. R.C. Zaehner (Dent, London, 1966): p.20
The Concise Encyclopedia of Islam, ed. Cyril Glasse (Stacey International, London, 1989): p.13 (Qur'an extract)
The Holy Qur'an, trans. and commentary by Addullah Yusaf Ali (Lahore, 1934; facsimile edition by Islamic Propagation Centre International, Birmingham): extracts from the Qur'an
The Sacred Writings of the Sikhs, trans. Dr Trilochan Singh, Bhai Jodh Singh, Kapur Singh, Bawa Harkishen Singh, Khushwant Singh (Allen & Unwin, London, 1960): p.14
Translations of the Guru Granth Sahib are based on the version by Gurbachan Singh Talib (Punjabi University, 1984): pp.23, 53

Designed, typeset and illustrated by Topics – The Creative Partnership, Exeter

Printed in Great Britain by St Edmundsbury Press, Bury St Edmunds for SCM-Canterbury Press Ltd, Norwich

Contents

	Introduction	4
1	Quote, Unquote	7
2	The Golden Rule	16
3	Hot-Seat	25
4	Belonging	28
5	Treasures	33
6	Collage	44
7	Nativity	54
8	Pilgrimage	60
9	Moving Pictures	63
10	Afterthoughts	66

Introduction

The title says it all – or most of it. Whilst the tendency of many published RE materials for students aged 14 to 16 is to create a teaching and learning experience rooted in the use of a specific resource – a coursebook, a CD-ROM, a website – *REACT* simply provides access (with support for teachers and students) to a wide range of lively, provocative and stimulating classroom-based activities which use and develop the skills, understanding and awareness that students naturally bring to their work in RE.

Providing these sorts of activities is the essential stuff of good RE practice, of course. And having a core repertoire of tried and tested classroom approaches is what our work as RE teachers relies upon. Even the most experienced and inventive of us pick up and experiment with new ideas when we come across them – especially when, as here, they arrive in a ready-to-use format! And for newly qualified and non-specialist teachers, access to a store of RE activities for students aged 14 to 16 that are described and presented in detail is not only a helpful first step towards developing a bigger personal range but an important way of underpinning early success and confidence in the RE classroom.

REACT is not a random compendium of activities, though. One of the difficulties of delivering continuity and progression in RE is ensuring a planned approach to the development of relevant skills; too often the focus remains on the explicit and more easily managed issues of content. In a recent review of RE and agreed syllabuses across a cross-section of schools in England, Ofsted found that entirely separate groups of pupils in years 3, 6, 8 and 9 (ages 7, 10, 12 and 13) had been given the task of producing a visual account of the six biblical days of creation. In reviewing this work, it concluded that 'the only difference in outcome ... was in the quality of the art work'.

REACT focuses on creating practical opportunities for students to use and develop skills that are appropriate to RE. Skills frequently used in RE at ages 14 to 16 include research, interpretation, analysis, discussion, reflection and evaluation. Although some of these skills may also be encountered in other curriculum areas, the nature of RE puts them in a special context, giving them a distinctive purpose and character. This volume of *REACT* concentrates on two skills that are essential to quality work in RE at ages 14 to 16: reflection and evaluation. It provides a range of opportunities for students to identify, reflect upon and evaluate evidence, experience, ideas and issues to do with the spiritual and religious lives of themselves, other people and faith communities. Developing these particular skills is a dimension of RE regarded by Ofsted as a key action point for RE professionals. Its view of current practice is that 'while most pupils are learning a great deal about religions, few are being encouraged to learn from religion (SCAA AT2). Opportunities for reflection should be closely linked to the subject content. If there is not time for pupils to reflect on the meaning of what they study, evaluate moral issues or discuss their own developing beliefs and spirituality, then either the number of religions or the number of topics taught must be reduced. This is an issue both for schools and SACREs.'

Focusing on skills inevitably means that *REACT* does not deal systematically with content – after all, it is not a coursebook. However, the topics and themes it explores are selected appropriately from the requirements of SCAA model syllabuses, GCSE full and short courses, and the content of typical compulsory RE programmes and RE within PSE at ages 14 to 16. As well as being a ready-to-use classroom package, each activity is a process model, and the model is transferable in most cases to alternative content – from another religion or featuring a different topic. When considering transferability, do also consider issues of continuity and progression. You may find that some activities, possibly with modification, are equally suited to work you are doing with students aged 11 to 13 or 16+.

[Quotations are from *The impact of new agreed syllabuses on the teaching and learning of religious education*, Ofsted, 1997]

THE ACTIVITIES

Each activity assumes a class size of 30 pupils. A 'lesson' is always assumed to be a continuous single session of about 60 minutes' duration.

Explanations, instructions and supporting materials are presented in a standard sequence. This may include any or all of the following, as appropriate:

Overview	introduces and summarizes the activity, its purpose and content.
Objectives	are stated as learning outcomes.
Materials needed	is a full list. Do check it carefully. We have provided photocopiable resources where these would otherwise have to be specially prepared by you, but *REACT* activities may rely just as heavily on other materials that you will need to source from within school. Each type is listed separately.
Your role as teacher	This differs from activity to activity. The role the activity asks you to adopt as class teacher will influence the appropriateness of interactions in the classroom and the effectiveness of the learning that takes place there.
Classroom environment	is another important factor influencing interactions in the classroom, and it is worth taking the time to get this right. Like your role as teacher, setting up a particular environment will help establish a focus that is suited to the activity you are doing and the skills it is aiming to develop.
The activity step by step	provides detailed, easy-to-follow instructions and advice.
Adapting the activity	suggests ways of modifying the core activity to allow it to cater for the needs of students who are more able or whom you consider may have difficulty.
Homework	has ideas for work that can be done by students individually to extend or consolidate skills that have been encountered in the activity. In some cases, the homework may be preparation for the next stage of the activity.
Extending the activity	gives ideas for further classroom work linked to the activity.
Changing the focus	gives suggestions for suitable alternative topics or issues to use with the activity.
Photocopiable materials	are provided at the end of each activity, where required. Also check the list of *Materials needed* for the activity you are planning to use.

1 Quote, Unquote

Overview

As one of the few questions in RE which young people of any age can engage with, 'What is God?' is almost a benchmark. The responses it stimulates give useful insight into the underlying skills, attitudes and experience which students are bringing to their work in RE.

'What is God?' is also in many ways deceptively familiar territory. All students will have at some point considered the question for themselves – and probably formally, too, as part of earlier learning in RE – so there is no shortage of personal reflections and assumptions to be found in their work.

However, having and articulating a personal idea of God is one thing; being able to reflect upon and evaluate a range of other people's ideas of God is another. *Quote, Unquote* is about evidence. Some of the evidence used in this activity is personal view, much of it is scriptural authority; all of it represents a range of belief and opinion. Students discover that by drawing on skills and materials rather than just feelings and hunches, a question like 'What is God?' can be answered clearly, with insight and with the authority of scriptural evidence.

Objectives

By the end of this activity, students should be able to reflect upon and evaluate the qualities which people attribute to God.

Materials needed

Photocopiable
- *Children's Ideas about God* (pp.9–11) – 1 set of 3 sheets per pair
- *Statements about God* (p.12) – 1 sheet for you as teacher
- *Quotations about God* (pp.13–14) – 1 set of 2 sheets per pair
- *Characteristics of God* (p.15) – 1 sheet per pair

Other
- Drawing paper – 1 sheet per student
- Masking tape for display purposes – 1 short piece per student
- A4 writing paper – 1 sheet per pair
- Reference books for more-able students' research work about ideas of God in different religious traditions

Your role as teacher
- Organizer
- Reader
- Discussion leader

Classroom environment

Arrange the room to allow students to work in pairs and move around the edge of the room. Clear wall space for display – this will be needed during the activity.

Quote, Unquote

The activity step by step

1 Provide each student with one sheet of drawing paper then organize this opening task:
(i) Working individually, students take on the role of a six-year-old primary-school pupil and – from this imaginary perspective – draw 'what God is like' and write words about God around their pictures or write a short description of God in words. (For Muslim or Jewish children the latter would be more appropriate.)
(ii) When they have finished, they display their own work on the wall space provided then view all the work, looking for similarities in the images and words used.

2 Lead a short discussion on recurring ideas about characteristics of God in the display of work.

3 Organize this task:
Students work in pairs. Each pair is given a set of *Children's Ideas about God* sheets (pages 9–11) and one sheet of A4 writing paper. On the paper they list the qualities of God which the children describe.

4 With the whole class, summarize on the board the qualities and characteristics of God collected so far.

5 Organize these tasks:
(i) Ask the students to have their lists in front of them, then read out to the whole class qualities and characteristics of God from the sheet *Statements about God*. When they identify an idea which matches a quality or characteristic in their lists, they tick it. They also add to their lists any new ideas.
(ii) Working in their previous pairs, students are now given the chart *Characteristics of God*. Referring to their lists of qualities and characteristics of God, they write in the left-hand column of the chart the qualities and characteristics they consider most important.
   Next, students receive a set of *Quotations about God* sheets. They should consider each extended quotation in turn and decide which of the qualities or characteristics of God they have listed in their charts it refers to. In the appropriate faith column in their charts, students place a tick against each quality or characteristic they identify.

Adapting the activity

For less-able students
Run the activity as described up to stage 5(i). Less-able students will need your help in order to interpret the evidence used at stage 5(ii). This stage could be managed as a whole-class activity, with each student having a chart of their own in front of them. Alternatively, students working in pairs could be given a version of the chart with your selection of suitable 'Characteristics/Qualities' listed in the left-hand column.

For more-able students
Run the activity as described up to stage 5(i). From this point, ask more-able students to research appropriate quotations about God from different religious traditions and to devise their own chart for analysing them.

Homework

Ask students to write a statement based on ideas generated through the class activity. The statement begins 'God is … '

Changing the focus

A similar activity could be based around ideas about (i) death or (ii) Heaven and Hell.

Children's Ideas about God

With thanks to the pupils of Boringdon Primary School, Plympton

'God's like my daddy with a beard and a moustache. He's kind and tells jokes and lives in heaven in a tree-house. God is a 'he' – I've known that since I was a baby.'

Sebastian, aged 4

'God sees everything in the sky. He's very high up and he's got bigger eyes than us.'

Rhys, aged 6

'God is everywhere, so I suppose we're sitting on him. You can feel God.'

Kirsty, aged 6

'I believe in God and I go to church every Sunday. I feel safe as I'm in God's family. I pray to God and talk to him about people who are dead or alive and sick. Sometimes I pray for my friends if they're in trouble.'

Jessica, aged 8

Children's Ideas about God

At first God made a good world but so many people have ruined it so God is cross and he could make sure there isn't a good harvest.

Amy, aged 10

I think God's everyone's spirit. When it's raining he's crying because something's happened to people he likes. When it's thunder he's angry. When it's sunny he's happy. When it's cloudy he's coughed! I picture him all the time when I'm in bed.

Nicholas, aged 10

I don't exactly think that God made the world because there are other scientific ideas, but I think there might be someone or something out there that we call God.

Simon, aged 10

I believe in God because if I didn't there wouldn't be any galaxies or stars or planets. Without them there'd be just pitch black without anything in it.

Robbie, aged 8

Children's Ideas about God

I believe in God because of nature and animals – trees and rabbits. I don't think God's very happy if we destroy things but he might forgive us.

Nicholas, aged 8

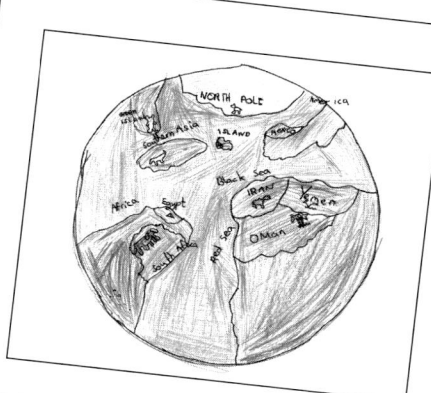

I believe in God because how else could the world be here? Without him there would be no life. I think it's a good world.

Charlotte, aged 8

God is kind to people and helps them get better. He knows if they're poorly. God is air.

Stuart, aged 6

I reckon there is a God. When he's angry he makes diseases. I reckon God can do anything.

Daniel, aged 10

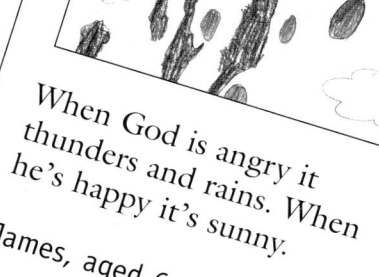

When God is angry it thunders and rains. When he's happy it's sunny.

James, aged 6

Statements about God

Note to teachers
This sheet contains six statements summarizing the principal ideas of God across the six major religious traditions. They have been organized like this to help you with your planning, and also to keep them contextualized. We do not recommend presenting these ideas to students out of context.

These are some of the principal ideas of God held by people who belong to the world's main religions.

Buddhists	believe that there is no supreme, personal being.
Christians	believe that there is one God who is the creator and the redeemer. They believe that God is the Father, the Son and the Holy Spirit (three persons in one – the Trinity). To Christians, God is omnipotent (all-powerful), righteous, all-loving, just, almighty, holy and forgiving.
Hindus	believe that God is the ultimate reality, it, the world-soul, taking many forms, and manifested through avatars (the bodily form of a deity who has descended to earth). They believe that, like salt in brine, God is invisible yet all-pervasive. God is in the soul of every person, in everything that exists, and eternal. To understand God is to understand one's real self.
Muslims	believe that there is one God (Allah) who is the creator and the giver of life. They believe that God is compassionate and merciful. God is a guide, rewards good and punishes evil, and has pre-knowledge.
Jews	believe that there is one God who is the creator. They believe that God is without form or body, the first and the last. God rewards the good, punishes the wicked and resurrects the dead.
Sikhs	believe that there is one God who is the creator. They believe that God is invisible, in every form of life, immanent (present throughout the universe), personal and loving. God is eternal truth and fears nothing. The body is God's temple.

Quotations about God

ISLAM

He is God;
There is no god but He.
He is the Knower of the Unseen and the Visible;
He is the All-merciful, the All-compassionate.
He is God;
There is no god but He.
He is the King, the All-holy, the All-peaceable,
the All-faithful, the All-preserver,
the All-mighty, the All-compeller,
the All-sublime.
Glory be to God, above that they associate!
He is God,
the Creator, the Maker, the Shaper.
To Him belong the Names Most Beautiful.
All that is in the heavens and the earth magnifies Him;
He is the All-mighty, the All-wise.

Qur'an 59:22–24

HINDUISM

Imperishable is the Lord of Love.
As from a blazing fire thousands of sparks
Leap forth, so millions of beings arise
From the Lord of Love and return to him.

The Lord of Love is above name and form.
He is present in all and transcends all.
Unborn, without body and without mind,
He is the source of space, air, fire and water,
And the earth that holds us all.

Fire is his head, the sun and moon his eyes,
The heavens his ears, the scriptures his voice,
The air his breath, the universe his heart,
And the earth his footrest. The Lord of Love
is the innermost Self of all.

Mundaka Upanishad II:1:1-4

Quotations about God

SIKHISM There is one God,
Eternal Truth is his Name;
Maker of all things,
Fearing nothing and at enmity with nothing.
Timeless is his Image;
Not begotten, being of his own Being:
By the grace of the Guru, made known to men.

Adi Granth 1 (the Mool Mantar)

CHRISTIANITY "This is how you should pray:
'Our Father in heaven:
May your holy name be honoured;
may your kingdom come;
may your will be done on earth as it is in heaven.
Give us today the food we need.
Forgive us the wrongs we have done,
as we forgive the wrongs that
others have done to us.
Do not bring us to hard testing,
but keep us safe from the Evil One.'
If you forgive others the wrongs they have done to you, your Father in heaven will also forgive you; but if you do not forgive others, then your Father will not forgive the wrongs you have done."

Matthew 6:9–14

JUDAISM The Lord, the Lord, the compassionate
and gracious God, slow to anger,
abounding in love and faithfulness,
maintaining love to thousands, and
forgiving wickedness, rebellion and sin.
Yet he does not leave the guilty
unpunished; he punishes the children
and their children for the sin of
the fathers to the third and fourth
generation.

Exodus 34:6–7

Characteristics of God

QUALITIES AND CHARACTERISTICS	✝	ॐ	☪	✡	☬

2 The Golden Rule

Overview

When students talk about the things they find offputting about religion, many identify what they consider to be the outdated and quirky set of dos and don'ts. Equipping students with the skills and confidence to reflect upon and evaluate religious law is an important part of developing their understanding of religion. Yet faced with the prospect of student resistance to an intransigent topic, it is easy to find good reasons not to tackle it.

Remember that, for many students, rules are not just a topic, they are an issue. Develop the issue alongside the content and you add a dimension which can animate classroom activity and lead students towards some important insights. If your own experience of RE as a student is clouded by memories of having to learn the Ten Commandments by heart, try this activity as therapy!

The Golden Rule introduces students to religious laws from the major faith traditions as rules for living. Students consider the areas of life covered by religious rules and whether there are different types of rule. They have opportunities to reflect on why religious rules exist and the extent to which these rules agree on what constitutes behaviour worthy of human beings.

Objectives

By the end of this activity students should be able to:

- describe some laws from the religions selected for study;
- explain how religious laws can influence everyday behaviour;
- reflect on and evaluate the connection between religious law and the Golden Rule.

Materials needed

Photocopiable
- *Religions Board* (p.18) – 1 sheet per pair
- *Law Cards* (pp. 19–23) – 1 set per pair
- *Hillel Story/Fundamental Laws* (p.24) – 1 sheet for you as teacher

Other
None

Your role as teacher

- Organizer
- Reader
- Discussion leader

Classroom environment

Arrange the furniture to allow small groups to work around tables.

The Golden Rule

The activity step by step

1 Organize this opening task:
Working in pairs, students are given one set of *Law Cards* and one *Religions Board*. They sort the cards by placing them where they think they belong on the board. (Alternatively you may prefer to cut the *Religions Board* into separate cards and ask students to place the appropriate *Law Cards* underneath them.)

2 With the whole class, go through the correct sorting of the cards. (Note that the quotations from the Hebrew Bible relate to Judaism, not Christianity, in this activity.) As you do this, the pairs should mark on each of their cards, for recognition only, the symbol of the religion to which it belongs. (Symbols are shown on the *Religions Board* in a simplified form for easy copying.)

3 Organize this task:
Pairs join together into groups of four. In these groups, students discuss other possible ways of grouping the cards (e.g. according to the things they refer to, such as food, personal behaviour, social behaviour) and resort them into new categories.

4 With the whole class, collect new categories of ideas and write these on the board. Discuss with the class what constitutes a religious code of behaviour.

5 Read to the class the *Hillel Story* and examples of *Fundamental Laws* in different religious traditions (page 24).

6 Now introduce the class to the concept of the Golden Rule.

7 Organize these tasks:
(i) In the same groups of four, students select several law cards from different religious traditions which they feel are a good interpretation of the Golden Rule.
(ii) Each group chooses one of the laws it has selected, and appoints a spokesperson to explain to the class why this law is a good interpretation of the Golden Rule.
(iii) With the whole class, listen to the presentations from the spokespeople.

> **Note to teachers**
> The Rehat Maryada is a code of discipline which is binding only upon Khalsa Sikhs. However, other Sikhs who are not amritari Sikhs will also follow these commandments.

Adapting the activity

For less-able students
At stage 3, supply categories. Keep these simple (e.g. food, home, family).

For more-able students
Limit or omit guidance about possible alternative categories when setting up stage 3. At stage 7, ask the students to produce their own written summary of the laws which reflect the Golden Rule.

Homework

Ask students to note examples of people's behaviour during the following week – on television, in newspapers, at home, at school – then to list these according to (a) whether they follow the Golden Rule or (b) whether they break the Golden Rule.

Religions Board

HINDUISM	SIKHISM
CHRISTIANITY	**JUDAISM**
BUDDHISM	**ISLAM**

Law Card

May all beings be at ease.
Let none deceive another
Or despise any being in any state;
Let none through anger or ill-will
Wish harm upon another,
Even as a mother
Protects with her life
Her child, her only child,
So with a boundless heart
Should we cherish all living things,
Radiating kindness
Over the entire world –
Upwards to the skies
And downwards to the depths,
Outward and unbounded.
Free from hatred and ill-will,
Whether walking or standing,
Seated or lying down,
Free from drowsiness,
One should sustain this recollection.

Suttanipata I:8
(The Discourse on Loving Kindness)

Law Card

Do not think lightly of evil, saying: 'It will not come to me'. Even as a water-pot is filled by the falling of drops, likewise the fool, gathering it drop by drop, fills himself with evil.

Do not think lightly of good, saying: 'It will not come to me'. Even as a water-pot is filled by the falling of drops, so the wise man, gathering it drop by drop, fills himself with good.

Dhammapada

Law Card

My commandment is this: love one another, just as I love you. The greatest love a person can have for his friends is to give his life for them.

John 15:12 – 13

Law Card

Hatred is never appeased by hatred in this world; it is appeased by love. This is an eternal truth.

Dhammapada

Law Card

I undertake the rule of training to refrain from taking that which is not given.

From the Five Precepts
(Second Precept)

Law Card

Say to the believing men
That they should lower
Their gaze and guard
Their modesty: that will make
For greater purity for them:
And God is well acquainted
With all that they do.

And say to the believing women
That they should lower
Their gaze and guard
Their modesty; that they
Shall not display their
Beauty and ornaments except
What must ordinarily appear
Thereof.

Qur'an 29:30–31

Law Card

He who seeks happiness must strive
for contentment and self-control.
Happiness arises from contentment;
uncontrolled pursuit of wealth will
result in unhappiness.

Manusmriti 4:2

Law Card

You must perform your bounden Duty,
for action is better than idleness.

Bhagavad Gita 3:8

Law Card

Do not neglect your duties to the gods
and ancestors.
Let your mother be a god to you.
Let your father be a god to you.
Let your teacher be a god to you.
Let a guest be a god to you.

Taittriya Upanishad 1:11:2

Law Card

Look then to your proper Duty
and you will have no cause for fright,
soldiers have nothing better here
than Duty that demands a fight.

But if you neglect this conflict
which Duty says you must fulfil
abandoning your proper Duty
and honour you will come to ill.

Krishna in the Bhagavad Gita 2:31–33

Law Card

Do not take revenge on someone who wrongs you. If anyone slaps you on the right cheek, let him slap you on the left cheek too. And if someone takes you to court to sue you for your shirt, let him have your coat as well.

Matthew 5:39–40

Law Card

Do not worry about your life, what you will eat; or about your body, what you will wear. Life is more than food, and the body more than clothes.

Luke 12: 22–23

Law Card

Let not some men
Among you laugh at others:
It may be that
The latter are better
Than the former:
Nor let some women
Laugh at others:
It may be that
The latter are better
Than the former:
Nor defame nor be
Sarcastic to each other,
Nor call each other
By offensive nicknames …

Qur'an 49:11

Law Card

Do not judge others, so that God will not judge you, for God will judge you in the same way as you judge others, and he will apply to you the same rules as you apply to others.

Matthew 7:1–2

Law Card

Do not store up riches for yourselves here on earth, where moths and rust destroy, and robbers break in and steal. Instead, store up riches for yourselves in heaven … For your heart will always be where your riches are.

Matthew 6:19–21

Law Card

You may eat any kind of fish that has fins and scales, but anything living in the water that does not have fins and scales must not be eaten.

Leviticus 11:9 – 10

Law Card

Be wise enough not to wear yourself out trying to get rich. Your money can be gone in a flash, as if it had grown wings and flown away like an eagle.

Proverbs 23:4 – 5

Law Card

Respect your father and your mother, so that you may live a long time in the land that I am giving you.
Do not commit murder.
Do not commit adultery.
Do not steal.
Do not accuse anyone falsely.
Do not desire another man's house; do not desire his wife, his slaves, his cattle, his donkeys, or anything else that he owns.

Exodus 20:12 – 17

Law Card

Do not take advantage of anyone or rob him. Do not hold back the wages of some you have hired, not even for one night. Do not curse a deaf man or put something in front of a blind man so as to make him stumble over it.

Leviticus 19:13 – 14

Law Card

Do not take life – which God
Has made sacred – except
For just cause.

Qur'an 17:31

Law Card

Do not make a promise in my name if you do not intend to keep it; that brings disgrace on my name. I am the Lord your God.

Leviticus 19:11

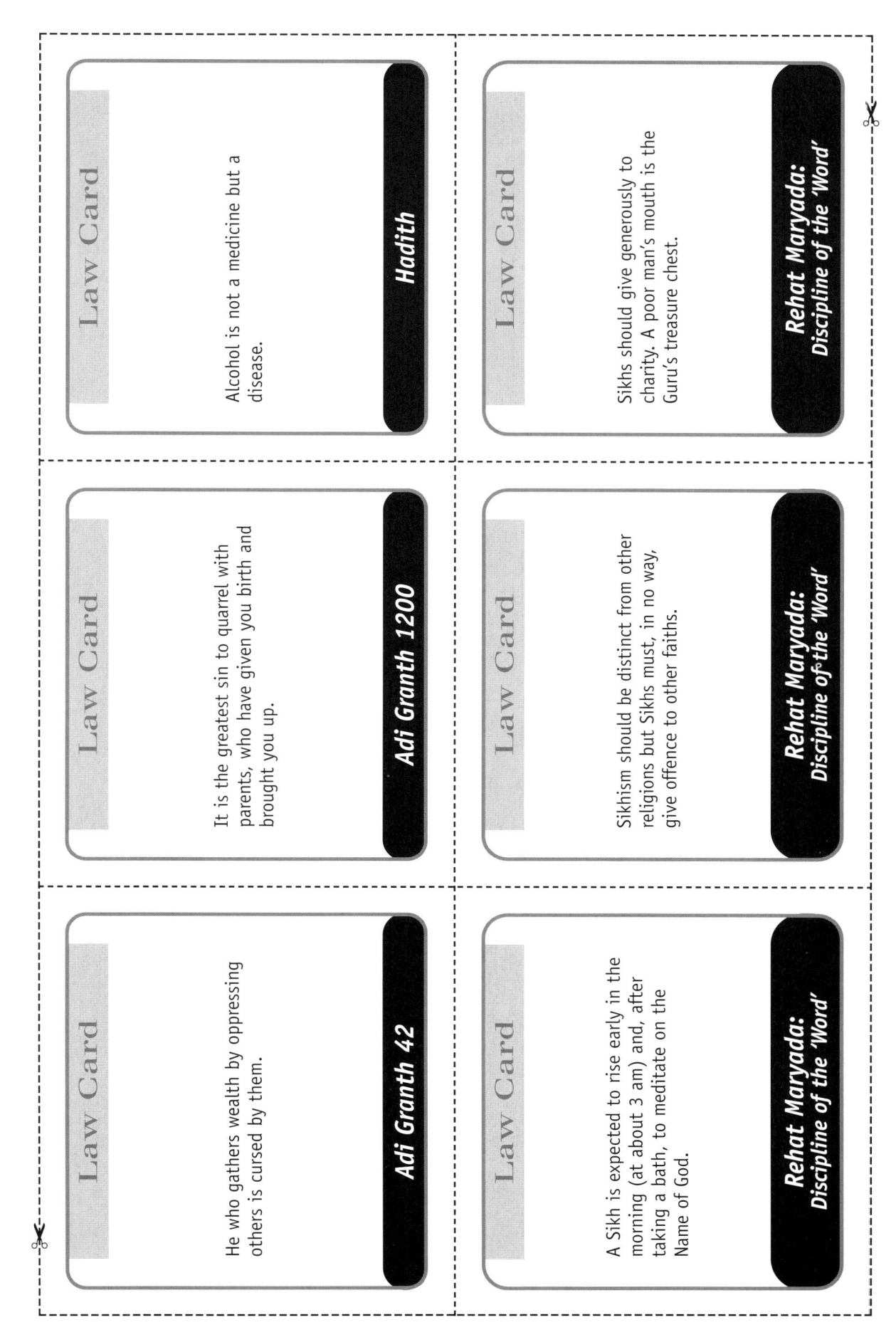

Law Card

He who gathers wealth by oppressing others is cursed by them.

Adi Granth 42

Law Card

It is the greatest sin to quarrel with parents, who have given you birth and brought you up.

Adi Granth 1200

Law Card

Alcohol is not a medicine but a disease.

Hadith

Law Card

A Sikh is expected to rise early in the morning (at about 3 am) and, after taking a bath, to meditate on the Name of God.

Rehat Maryada:
Discipline of the 'Word'

Law Card

Sikhism should be distinct from other religions but Sikhs must, in no way, give offence to other faiths.

Rehat Maryada:
Discipline of the 'Word'

Law Card

Sikhs should give generously to charity. A poor man's mouth is the Guru's treasure chest.

Rehat Maryada:
Discipline of the 'Word'

Hillel Story/Fundamental Laws

Rabbi Hillel and the Golden Rule

One of the most learned Jewish teachers was Rabbi Hillel. This story is told about him.

One day towards the end of his life, when he was old and infirm, Rabbi Hillel was paid a visit by a man who had heard about his great knowledge and wisdom. The man, who wasn't Jewish, said he would consider becoming a Jew if Hillel could teach him the whole of the Torah while standing on one leg.

Rabbi Hillel led the man into his large study. Every wall was covered in bookshelves, and every shelf was groaning with sacred or scholarly books. The Rabbi gestured at the books and sighed. Then he turned to the man and looked him straight in the eye.

'Yes, I can certainly teach you the Torah in the time I can bear to stand as you wish,' he said.

Hillel painfully raised himself on to one leg then took one long, deep breath. 'And this is what it says: "What is hateful to you, do not do to your neighbour." That is the whole of the Torah. The rest is commentary.'

'Now,' said Hillel to the man, 'go and learn it.'

Fundamental Laws

The Golden Rule is that you should always treat others as you would like them to treat you. This is how the six major religions express it:

Buddhism	I will act towards others exactly as I would act towards myself. *Udama-Varga, c.500 BCE*
Christianity	So in everything, do to others what you would have them do to you, for this sums up the Law and the Prophets. *St Matthew's Gospel 7:12, c.65 CE*
Hinduism	This is the sum of duty: Do nought to others which, if done to you, could cause you pain. *Mahabharata, c.50 BCE*
Islam	None of you 'truly' believe until he wishes for his brother what he wishes for himself. *Saying of Muhammad, seventh century CE*
Judaism	What is harmful to yourself do not do to your fellow men. This is the whole truth of the law and the remainder is but commentary. *Hillel: Talmud c.100 CE*
Sikhism	As you deemst yourself, so deem others. Cause suffering to no-one. Thereby return to your True Home with honour. *Guru Granth Sahib, 1604 CE*

3 Hot-Seat

Overview

One of the difficulties with open issues-based discussion in the classroom is that, although it offers an arena in which students can articulate their views, it provides few opportunities for those ideas to be developed. Vigorous discussion in particular often leads to participants becoming defensive, and this not only hardens the views they present but can make those views more extreme and uncompromising.

Hot-Seat offers a controlled environment for students to reflect upon, express and evaluate viewpoints to do with an issue. It ensures that a wide range of viewpoints is considered and puts students in a position where they may have to research and advocate a point of view alien to their own. It also allows all students – not just the most vocal – to take part.

The ultimate goal of *Hot-Seat* is to explore issues on which there is a range of moral, ethical and social viewpoints, including viewpoints held by faith communities. This is not achieved in one step, though. You will need to assess the skills, maturity and confidence of the class as it approaches the task of presenting, interrogating and understanding deeply held views. We offer three *Hot-Seat* suggestions to get you started (see page 27).

Objectives

By the end of this activity, students should be able to:

- explain the main viewpoints within the issue(s) explored;
- reflect upon and evaluate why these viewpoints may be adopted.

Materials needed

Photocopiable
None

Other
Students will need access to reference materials for their research on the issue(s).

Your role as teacher

- Organizer
- During the activity: either representing a viewpoint in the 'hot-seat' or observing

Classroom environment

Push back tables and desks to allow room to arrange chairs in a circle.

Hot-Seat

The activity step by step

1 **Preparation:**
Proper preparation with the students in advance is essential for this activity. In an earlier lesson:
(i) Agree with the students the issue(s) which will be the activity's focus. Identify some of the viewpoints that people may have on the issue(s). (Subject-areas for issues and ranges of viewpoints are suggested on page 27.)
(ii) Let the students appoint a chairperson.
(iii Divide the rest of the class into (or allow students to choose between being) contenders for the 'hot-seat' (about six contenders required) and an audience with prepared questions. (Sample questions are given on page 27.)
(iv) Decide which viewpoints the contenders for the hot-seat are going to represent.
   All students will need time for research. The hot-seaters also have to consider the background to their viewpoint on the issue and the audience their questions. The chairperson should prepare a brief introduction.

2 **On the day:**
Once responsibilities and roles have been allocated, this activity is largely self-organizing. Explain the following structure to the students and, if necessary, discreetly help the chairperson keep to it.
(i) The chairperson introduces the activity then invites the first hot-seater to take the chair.
(ii) In turn, hot-seaters are questioned by the audience on the chosen issue(s). The chairperson manages the order of questions and the time each hot-seater is allowed.
(iii) The chairperson draws the activity to a close and thanks the hot-seaters for their insights and contributions.

Adapting the activity

For less-able students
Chair the activity yourself. Give help during the preparation of questions, or supply questions, depending on need. Make sure hot-seaters feel ready and direct their research if necessary.

For more-able students
Allow students to choose their own theme, decide the six hot-seat viewpoints and make up the questions.

Homework

Ask students to describe as many of the viewpoints on the issue as they can remember and to comment on those with which they identify personally.

Extending the activity

In a subsequent lesson, introduce faith viewpoints into the exploration of issues. Invited guests from a faith community might be prepared to take the hot-seat, or students could research the issue(s) from faith-community perspectives and represent community viewpoints in the hot-seat.

Changing the focus

Any issue with several viewpoints would be suitable for *Hot-Seat*.

Hot-Seat

Suggested subject-areas for issues

You may prefer to identify the subject-area so as to keep within a scheme of work, but allow students to specify the issue, albeit with some guidance from you.

Before students work on an issue, it needs to be stated in clear and practical terms. Here is an example: 'A by-pass has been proposed to divert a major trunk road away from a busy town centre. Engineering and cost considerations mean there is just one possible route for it: across a designated area of outstanding landscape value.'

Focus: **An environmental issue** (e.g. road-building or agro-chemical pollution)

Viewpoints: Industrialist
Farmer
Animal-rights activist
Motorist
Member of an environmental pressure group
Secondary-school student

Focus: **An issue to do with war** (e.g. involvement in other nations' conflicts)

Viewpoints: Serving member of the armed forces
Conscientious objector
War veteran
War widow(er)
Refugee
British Prime Minister

Focus: **An issue to do with the developing world** (e.g. exploitation of workers)

Viewpoints: Aid worker
Importer of goods (e.g. textiles) from developing world
Travel agent
Factory worker in developing world
Journalist
Industrialist in developed world

Sample questions

What matters to you?
What would you be prepared to 'fight' for?
Who is important to you?
What's your involvement in this issue?
How are you affected by this issue?
How can you help others?
Should the world be aware of this issue?
Why should we listen to you?
Does the public have a part to play?

4 Belonging

Overview

Not all religions have a monastic tradition, but for those that do monasticism may have a major role to play, sometimes to the extent that understanding it is a key to understanding the religion itself.

To students, the concept of monasticism often seems bizarre. Aspects of monastic life, such as the discipline, self-sacrifice and retreat from the world, are alien to their own experience, making the whole phenomenon difficult to grasp. However, students do have relevant experience to draw on. They will already be members of several types of community, such as a family, school, club or village. They know a lot about how communities operate.

This activity begins by helping students identify and reflect on their own experience of community. Later, students draw up specifications for a community and match these against the factors that characterize a specifically religious community.

Objectives

By the end of this activity, students should be able to:

- explain the importance of belonging to a community;
- explain the concept of a religious community;
- reflect upon and evaluate what it means to belong to a religious community.

Materials needed

Photocopiable
- *Belonging* sheet (p.30) – 1 per student
- *Community Charter* (p.31) – 1 per group of six students
- *Community Charter: Headings* (p.32) – 1 OHP transparency
- *Community Charter: Examples of Activity* (p.32) – 1 OHP transparency (superimposes on *Community Charter: Headings*)

Other
- Overhead projector
- Suitable reference books to support students' research into key word(s) which denote concept(s) of religious community
- Paper – enough for each group to write its reflections on key words

Your role as teacher

- Organizer
- Discussion leader

Classroom environment

Arrange the tables to allow students to work in pairs and move easily into groups of six.

The activity step by step

1 Organize this opening task:
(i) Students work in pairs; each student is given one *Belonging* sheet.
(ii) Drawing on their own experience, paired students talk to each other about where in society they feel they belong and what gives them their

Belonging

feeling of belonging. (You may feel you need to give examples of groups or communities, such as 'family', 'club', 'team'.)

(iii) During this discussion, students refer to their *Belonging* sheet. They write under 'People can belong to ...' the groups that apply to them, then consider the trigger words listed under the headings 'Belonging gives people ...' and 'Belonging requires from people ...', adding new words or deleting existing ones in the light of ideas that come up.

2 With the whole class, discuss what it means to 'belong'. Allow the students to continue refining their lists of trigger words as a result of ideas that arise. At the end of the discussion, ask them to select the ten trigger words most applicable to how they feel personally about belonging.

3 Merge pairs to create groups of six. Distribute one *Community Charter* sheet to each group, then organize this task:
(i) Set the scene by suggesting that a community should be able to meet the needs of the individuals within it.
(ii) Using ideas that emerged during paired discussion and students' own top ten trigger words, each group negotiates what a community should be able to offer individuals within it and writes this up on its *Community Charter* sheet.

4 Put up the completed *Community Charter: Headings* OHP transparency and explain to the class that this shows some of the typical aims of a community. Superimpose on this the *Examples of Activity* OHP transparency, which introduces some of the ways in which religious communities meet these aims (e.g. guidance = teaching through scripture and worship; support = charity work; fun = families getting together at festival time). Discuss this and answer any questions.

5 Organize this task:
(i) Working in the same groups of six and using reference books, students research one of the following key words used to denote specific concepts of religious community in different religious traditions: vihara, ummah, langar, monastery or fellowship, hevrah kaddisha, ashram.
(ii) Groups reflect on the concept of community in religion and what this means to believers.

Adapting the activity

For less-able students
At stage 5, instead of looking at a concept of religious community, provide information about a specific community (e.g. the Benedictine monks at Buckfast Abbey, Devon). With the students, look at how individual members contribute to and benefit from their community involvement.

For more-able students
Organize an extra task. Students look for examples of the type of religious community they have been investigating and reflect on the issues the examples raise. (E.g. Is this type of community found in more than one religious tradition? Do the examples show consistency or variety, and what could this mean?)

Homework

A short evaluative essay: 'Could religion survive without religious communities?'

Changing the focus

Try extending the activity into work on what it means to be a Jew, Christian, Hindu, Muslim, Sikh, Buddhist. The *Faith and Commitment* series (RMEP) contains much first-hand evidence on this dimension, including personal descriptions by followers of each faith of their own sense of belonging.

Belonging

People can belong to

....

....

Belonging gives people

support

fun

a listening ear

confidence

Belonging requires from people

commitment

obeying rules

giving things up

Community Charter

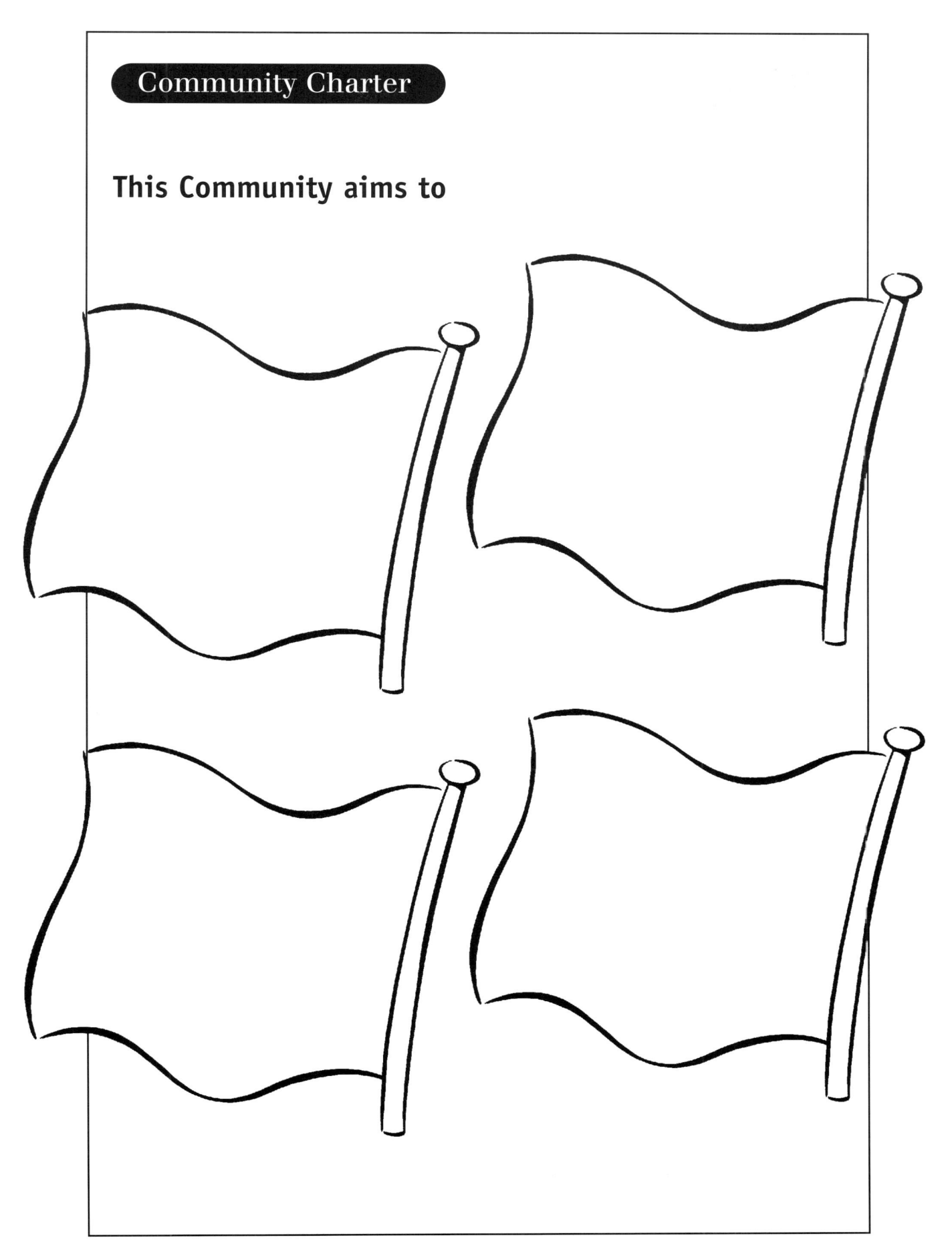

This Community aims to

Community Charter: Headings

- care
- offer a retreat
- support
- look outwards
- offer guidance
- tell others of its beliefs
- provide fun

Community Charter: Examples of Activity

- for the elderly – special needs
- – special quiet times
- its vulnerable members – counselling
- through charity work
- through teaching in scripture
- – through publicity
- – families get together at festivals and celebrations

32

5 Treasures

Overview

Religious communities are becoming increasingly concerned that outsiders place too much emphasis on the outward expression of faith, such as the artefacts used in prayer and worship. Certainly as far as RE is concerned, giving students technical information and language in areas like this does not automatically equip them to tackle questions of religious meaning and significance or help them to learn from religion; where too much technical information is introduced, it can sometimes be an obstacle to understanding.

In spite of this, the power of artefacts as a teaching and learning resource is unquestionable. Using pictures, *Treasures* is an activity which helps students reflect on some of the concepts underlying the use of artefacts in religion. The activity focuses first on artefacts as objects with a purpose, and students use their knowledge of religion to state clearly how they think several examples are used, or what they do. The focus then shifts to meaning. Students are given descriptions of the same artefacts in terms of their symbolism and significance and try to match artefact to description. Then they have to state clearly what they think each artefact contributes to prayer, worship or meditation. The challenge now is to find and use appropriate words.

Objectives

By the end of this activity, students should be able to:

- name and describe artefacts associated with prayer, worship and/or meditation in at least one religion;
- explain how those artefacts are used;
- reflect on what gives objects, actions, events and religious ritual significance.

Materials needed

Photocopiable
There are six different sheets of *Artefact pictures,* one per religion. Each sheet also contains artefact labels which should be cut off after photocopying. Matching each *Artefact pictures* sheet is a *Symbolism and significance* sheet. Faith symbols are used to help you keep these items co-ordinated in sets. For the religion(s) you are studying you will need:

- *Artefact pictures* (pp. 35–40) – one set per group
- *Symbolism and significance* (pp. 41–3) – one set per group

Other
- Reference books to provide information about prayer, worship and meditation in the religion(s) you are studying
- Large sheet of paper for displaying results of activity – one per group

Your role as teacher

- Organizer
- Discussion leader

Treasures

Classroom environment — Organize furniture so that students can work together in groups of four and move easily around the room.

The activity step by step

1 Organize this opening task:
(i) Students work in groups of four. Groups are given one set of artefacts pictures, showing artefacts from one religion. A heading on the sheet identifies the religion, but the artefacts themselves are unidentified and not shown in any context.
(ii) Groups look at the items on their sheets. First they discuss how these can be described in concrete or everyday terms, then they consider what sort of practical function, place or role the items might have in the religion.

2 Organize this task:
(i) Groups are now given the set of labels and the *Symbolism and significance* sheets that match the *Artefact pictures*.
(ii) By using the descriptions of symbolism and significance as their first information source and using reference books for any additional research, groups identify and label the items on their *Artefact pictures* sheet.

3 Organize this final task:
(i) Each group is given a large sheet of paper. Groups reflect on the items on their *Artefact pictures* sheets and agree words or phrases to describe what they think each item contributes to prayer, worship and/or meditation. The words are written under appropriate headings on the large sheet.
(ii) When all groups have done this, students circulate around the room to look at the words other groups have written.

4 With the whole class, lead a short discussion about finding words to describe the functions and meanings of religious artefacts. Explore similarities and differences in the words different groups have come up with.

Adapting the activity

For less-able students
With the students, label the artefact pictures before starting stage 2. The objective of stage 2 becomes finding out more about the named artefacts' meaning and purpose using the various information sources.

If you have access to any of the artefacts on which *Treasures* is based, less-able students in particular may benefit from being able to examine them in the classroom during this activity. Students should be reminded of the need to handle all religious artefacts with respect.

For more-able students
At stage 2, dispense with the artefact labels. Encourage students to identify the artefact pictures using only the descriptions of their symbolism and significance.

Homework — Ask the students to think about two artefacts which interested them and to write for someone with no previous knowledge a description of what they are, how they are used in prayer, worship and/or meditation and the special meaning or significance the artefacts and their use have for people of the faith community.

Alternatively, ask for a written evaluation of this statement: 'Worship requires the mind, body and spirit, not trinkets.'

Buddhism

image of Buddha	flowers
incense	prayer wheel
alms-bowl	robe
juzu (beads)	

Christianity

bread	candle
prayer-book	hymn-book
crucifix	vestment
incense	stoup
chalice (containing wine)	

Hinduism

om	arti lamp
incense	water
flower petals	food offering
kum kum powder	image
bell	conch shell
mala (prayer-beads)	scripture (Bhagavad Gita)

37

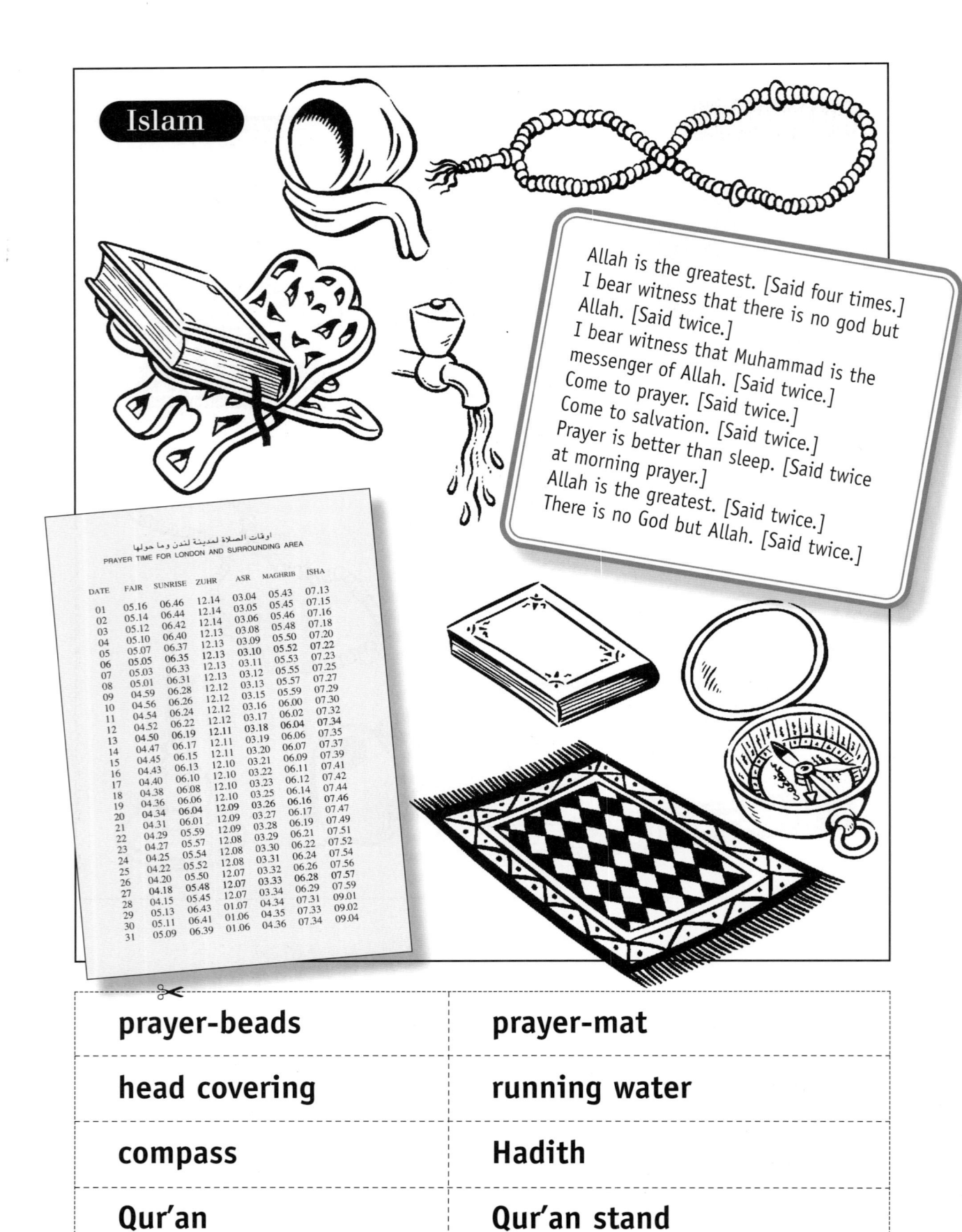

Islam

Allah is the greatest. [Said four times.]
I bear witness that there is no god but Allah. [Said twice.]
I bear witness that Muhammad is the messenger of Allah. [Said twice.]
Come to prayer. [Said twice.]
Come to salvation. [Said twice.]
Prayer is better than sleep. [Said twice at morning prayer.]
Allah is the greatest. [Said twice.]
There is no God but Allah. [Said twice.]

prayer-beads	prayer-mat
head covering	running water
compass	Hadith
Qur'an	Qur'an stand
adhan	prayer timetable

Judaism

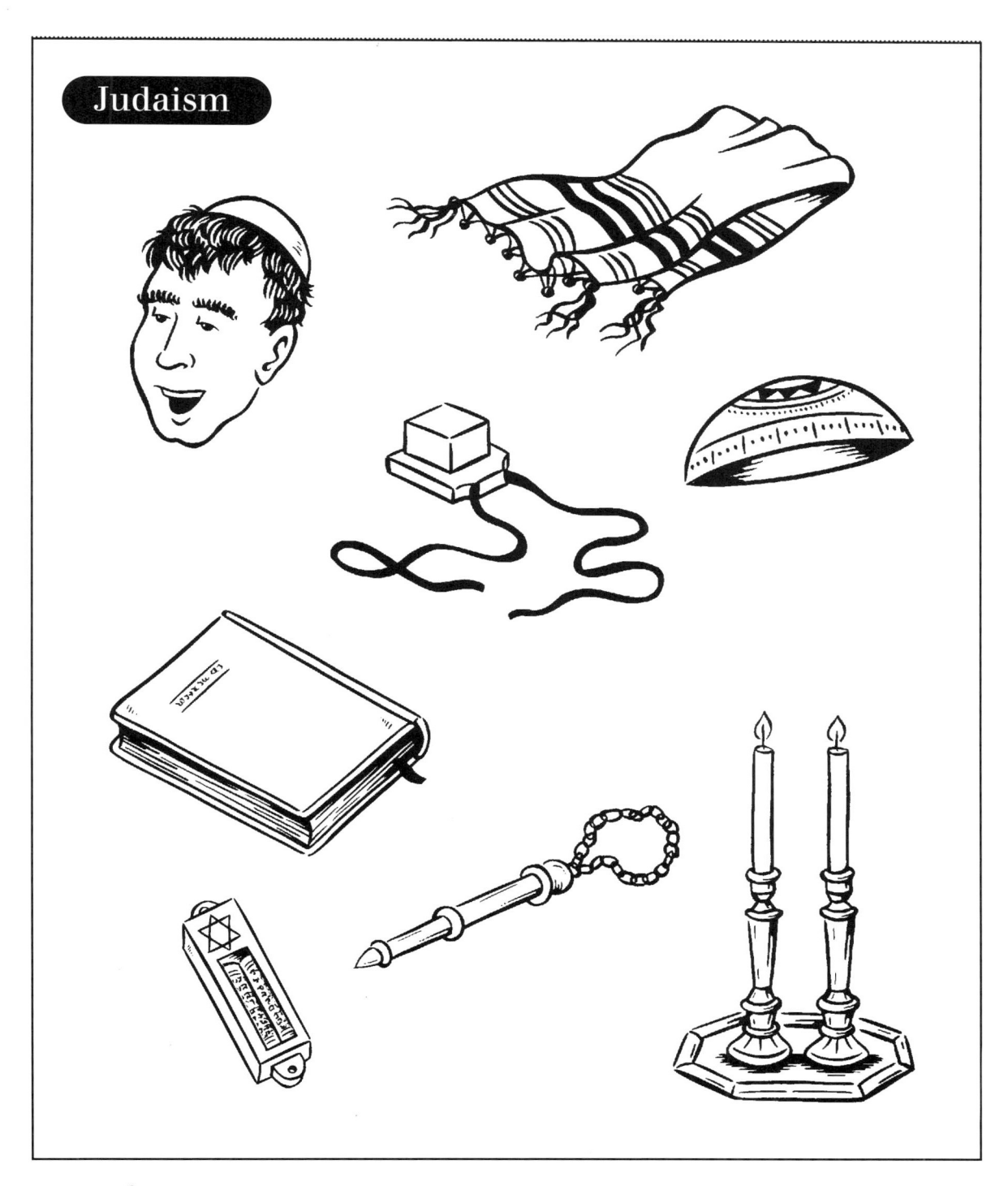

tefillin	tallit
yamulkah	mezuzah
yad	siddur
Shabbat candles	human voice

Sikhism

Guru Granth Sahib	chauri
bare feet	karah prashad
garland	picture of Guru (Nanak)
ik onkar	musical instrument
food and money offerings	

Symbolism and significance

Buddhism

A symbol of prayers.
An aid to meditation.
Produces aromatic smoke.

Garment, often saffron or maroon in colour. One of the few possessions a Buddhist monk or nun has.

Inscribed with prayers or sacred phrases. Turned by hand, wind or water.

Image of a person once thought by Buddhists to be too holy to depict. Now that his figure is shown, it is usually represented in positions of prayer, blessing or teaching.

Carried by Buddhist monks or nuns on their daily round to receive gifts of food from lay supporters.

Contains 108 beads. Used as an aid to concentration, to retain 'mindfulness'.

A fragrant aid to concentration.

Hinduism

A sweet offering made to a deity to invoke blessings. A symbol of prayers. Produces a purifying cloud of aromatic smoke.

Believed by Hindus to be the most sacred word in the universe. Said in worship, prayer, blessing and meditation.

Used to anoint deities during worship as an act of respect. When used on people, a symbol of God's blessing.

Essential to life. A symbol of life and one of the five elements out of which Hindus believe all things are made.

In the Bhagavad Gita, Krishna says, 'Whoever offers me, with devotion and a pure heart, a leaf, a flower, a fruit or a little water, I accept this offering.'

An offering of nourishment made to God. A sacrifice made as an expression of love.

Lit during worship to represent light. Contains fire – one of the five elements out of which Hindus believe all things are made.

Rung during worship to draw the attention and acknowledge the presence of God.

In a temple, a 'worshipful form' that invokes the presence of God. A specific form of God; Hindus believe in one God with many forms.

Blown at the beginning of the arti ceremony. Represents ether, one of the five elements out of which Hindus believe all things are made.

Contains 108 beads. Used in private prayer to help believers focus their concentration on the names of God.

The Song of God – Bhagavad Gita – is for many Hindus one of the most inspirational pieces of scripture and often kept close to hand.

Symbolism and significance

Judaism

Contains four biblical texts. Worn by men and boys over thirteen at morning prayers on weekdays. Fastened by straps to forehead and weaker arm.

Worn by men and boys over thirteen at morning services. A reminder of God's commandments.

Provides the only form of music allowed during Jewish worship. (As a sign of mourning after the destruction of the Temples in Jerusalem, instrumental music was banned.)

Used when reading from the Torah scrolls. Allows people to find their way in the text without having to touch the scrolls.

Book of daily Jewish prayer.

Contains biblical texts. Fastened to the main doorpost of Jewish homes. A reminder of God's commandments.

Lit by the mother of a Jewish household. Used to welcome in Shabbat.

Worn by men. A sign of humility and reverence towards God.

Islam

Used in private prayer. There are 99 beads, one for each of the 99 names of God mentioned in the Qu'ran.

Used to create a clean, sacred space for prayer. Allows Muslims to pray wherever they are at prayer times.

Wearing this is a sign of reverence and humility before God. Obligatory for men and women during worship and while reading the Qur'an.

Contains many sayings of and stories about the Prophet Muhammad. Second in authority only to the Qur'an.

Needed for ritual cleansing before prayer. Muslims must present themselves before God in a pure state.

Tells Muslims that it is time for them to pray.

Sacred scriptures revealed by God to the Prophet Muhammad. Treated with the utmost respect and handled with great care.

Helps Muslims in non-Muslim countries know the five daily times for salah (prayer). (The times depend on the position of the sun; the timetable shows these in local time around the world.)

Helps Muslims to pray correctly: that is, facing towards the Ka'bah in Makkah.

Used to raise the Qur'an above the floor as a sign of respect.

Symbolism and significance

Christianity

Symbol of Jesus as 'the light of the world'. Sometimes lit to symbolize prayers.

A symbol of prayers. An aid to meditation. Produces aromatic smoke.

Contains water which has been blessed. Found just inside the entrance to a church.

Contains wine which is consecrated at the Eucharist. When the wine is consecrated, some Christians believe it becomes the blood of Christ, others that it represents the blood of Christ.

Special garment worn by priests or officials during worship, sacred rituals and ceremonies.

Represents the death and suffering of Jesus.

The staff of life. When this is consecrated at the Eucharist, some Christians believe it becomes the body of Christ, others that it represents the body of Christ.

Contains words set to music for singing in public worship.

Contains the words of prayers used in communal worship.

Sikhism

Shows the founder of Sikhism, recalling his crucial teaching and example to the religion.

Often used to adorn the Guru Granth Sahib in recognition of its special status.

In countries like India people of importance and authority used to have servants to whisk away flies. During worship this item is waved continuously over the Guru Granth Sahib as a sign of respect.

Sikhs give these to the Guru Granth Sahib when they arrive at the gurdwara. They are used to help maintain the langar.

Given to everyone at the end of Sikh communal worship. A symbol of equality and sharing.

Hymn singing plays an important part in Sikh worship. Singing is accompanied by instruments such as sitars and tablas (drums).

A holy book and the embodiment of the Guru. The only Guru recognized by Sikhs since the death of Guru Gobind Singh in 1708. Must be present at all Sikh worship and ceremonies.

A sign of humility and respect during worship.

Two letters in Gurmukhi script which make up the Punjabi phrase 'God is One Being' – a key idea for Sikhs. Reminder of the Mool Mantar, which begins with this phrase.

43

6 Collage

Overview	'Building up a picture' is a metaphor we often use to describe the process of collecting, reflecting upon and evaluating evidence.
However, scriptural evidence can sometimes be difficult for students to evaluate. A particular reason is that the scriptures of the world's religions originated under and make reference to cultural and everyday conditions which are outside the experience of students in Britain at the start of the twenty-first century. To students, this cultural reference, and the language in which it is made, can either be an obstacle to them understanding the underlying message of religious scripture or, more often, make that message seem remote.
Collage is about evaluating scriptural evidence for its relevance to life today. To reinforce the contemporary dimension, the activity uses visual reminders of issues, attitudes and forms of behaviour that are part of modern living. Students reflect upon and evaluate scriptural extracts, interpreting each message, matching it with what they consider to be a relevant contemporary image, and gradually building a picture of the meaning of selected religious teachings in today's terms.
Objectives	By the end of this activity, students should be able to:
- describe the origin of some religious teachings;
- explain the possible variations in the interpretation of religious teachings;
- reflect on and evaluate the extent to which human behaviour may be influenced by religious teaching.
Materials needed	**Photocopiable**
- *Cartoons* (p. 47) – four copies per pair
- *Scriptural quotes* (pp. 48–53) – one set, relating to selected theme(s) and faiths (see 'The activity step by step' item 1), per pair

Other
- Scissors – one pair per pair
- Glue – one pot/tube per pair
- Paper – two large sheets per pair
- Felt-tip pen – one per pair
- Supply of magazines and newspapers (for work with more-able students) |
| **Your role as teacher** | - Organizer
- Discussion leader
- Reader |
| **Classroom environment** | Arrange tables for students to work in pairs, leaving space for students to move round the room to view the results of other pairs' work. |

Collage

The activity step by step

1 Preparation:
Look carefully at the *Scriptural quotes* sheets. These are organized by religion (six religions) and theme (four themes). Copy quotes for several themes from two or three religions or copy a selection from a wider range of faiths.

2 Organize this extended opening task:
(i) Students work in pairs. Each pair is equipped with two copies of the *Cartoon* sheets, a large sheet of paper, a pair of scissors, a felt-tip pen and glue.
(ii) Pairs divide their sheets of paper into two sections, heading one section 'Positive', the other 'Negative'.
(iii) Looking together at and discussing each image on the *Cartoon* sheet in turn, students decide whether the cartoon's message is a 'positive' or a 'negative' one. Having come to a view, they cut out the image and paste it on to the sheet under the appropriate heading, leaving space for a caption.
Pairs have two copies of each cartoon. If students feel a cartoon's message could be positive and negative, they can paste a copy under both headings.
(iv) Once all the cartoons have been looked at, categorized and pasted into place, students write a caption under each, describing the issue they think it depicts (e.g. pollution, crime, human rights, freedom of speech, peace, conflict).

Allow about 30 minutes for the task up to this point.

(v) At the end of the task, students circulate around the room to look at the work of other pairs. Ask students to look out for differences in the way pairs have interpreted the images.

3 Ask each pair to report back to the whole class one difference they noticed in the way a particular image had been interpreted. Allow this activity to develop into a discussion about how and why the same thing can have different meanings to different people.

4 Organize this activity:
(i) Students work in the same pairs as before. Each pair is given the set of *Scriptural quotes* you have selected and prepared, another large sheet of paper, another two copies of the *Cartoon* sheet, scissors and glue.
(ii) Pairs cut up and paste the scriptural quotes well-spaced across their sheet of paper. They then look at each cartoon in turn again to match the image with a quote. Having found a match, they cut out the image and paste it alongside the quote. (Some cartoons may match with several quotations or none, depending on the themes selected.)

5 Read the following quotation to the whole class:
> When God created the first man, he led him around all the trees in the Garden of Eden. He said to him, 'See my works, how beautiful and praiseworthy they are. Everything I have created has been created for your sake. Think of this, and do not corrupt or destroy my world; for if you corrupt it, there will be no one to set it right after you.'
> *A Jewish saying*

With the class, discuss what all the quotations mean and how they are relevant to everyday life today.

6 Organize this concluding task:
In pairs, students discuss the ancient teachings used in the lesson or other examples which they know, and particularly the relevance of these to the present time. This work is preparation for a homework activity.

Collage

Adapting the activity

For less-able students
Select and limit the number of scriptural quotes you provide.

For more-able students
Invite students to select their own cartoon images from magazines and newspapers to match with the scriptural quotes.

Homework

Set a piece of evaluative writing: 'Can ancient religious teachings be relevant to life today?'

Changing the focus

Different themes could be explored or the viewpoints of a wider range of faiths considered, depending on your original selection.

Collage Cartoons

Buddhism — Scriptural Quotes

The Natural World/Reverence for Life

Buddhism is a religion of love, understanding and compassion, and committed towards the ideal of non-violence. As such, it also attaches great importance to wildlife and the protection of the environment on which every human being in this world depends for survival.
Declaration of Assisi, 1986

Just as with her own life a mother shields from hurt her own, her only child, let all-embracing thoughts for all that lives be thine, an all-embracing love for all the universe in all its heights and depths and breadth, unstinted in love, unmarred by hate within, not rousing enmity.
Suttanipata (The Discourse on Loving Kindness)

I undertake the rule of training to refrain from harming any living things.
From The Five Precepts (First Precept)

Body Matters

I undertake the rule of training to refrain from taking drugs or drinks which tend to cloud the mind.
From The Five Precepts (Fifth Precept)

Better it were to swallow a ball of iron, red-hot and flaming, than to lead a wicked and unrestrained life eating the food of the people.
Dhammapada

Crime and Punishment

Though one man conquer a thousand times a thousand men in battle, he who conquers himself is the greatest warrior.
Dhammapada

All men fear pain and death, all men love life. Remembering that he is one of them, let a man neither strike nor kill.
Dhammapada

Hatred does not cease by hatred; hatred ceases only by love. This is the eternal truth.
Dhammapada

War and Peace

Generating one moment of love for one being is greater than making an ocean of offerings to a thousand Buddhas for a thousand years.
The Buddha

Do not harm others. Just as you feel affection on seeing a dearly beloved person, so you should extend loving kindness to all creatures.
The Buddha

Christianity — Scriptural Quotes

The Natural World/Reverence for Life

Aren't five sparrows sold for two pennies? Yet not one sparrow is forgotten by God.
Luke 12:6

Body Matters

Don't you know that your body is the temple of the Holy Spirit?
1 Corinthians 6:19

Do you know that you yourselves are God's temple and that God's spirit lives within you? If anyone destroys God's temple, God will destroy him, for God's temple is sacred and you are that temple.
1 Corinthians 3:16–17

Crime and Punishment

Do not repay anyone evil for evil.
Romans 12:17

Do not judge, or you too will be judged.
Matthew 7:1

All who take up the sword will die by the sword.
Matthew 26:52

War and Peace

Happy are those who work for peace, God shall call them his children.
Matthew 5:9

You have learned that it was said 'an eye for an eye, a tooth for a tooth.' But now I tell you: do not take revenge on someone who wrongs you. If anyone slaps you on the right cheek, let him slap your left cheek too.
Matthew 5:38–39

Everyone must obey the state authorities, because no authority exists without God's permission ... whoever opposes the existing authority opposes what God has ordered.
Romans 13:1–2

Do not think that I have come to bring peace to the world. No, I did not come to bring peace, but a sword.
Matthew 10:34

Hinduism — Scriptural Quotes

The Natural World/Reverence for Life

The earth has enough for every man's need, but not for every man's greed.
Mahatma Gandhi

Body Matters

He (man) must not get wilfully addicted to any object or substance or self gratification; he must try to overcome such dependence through willpower.
Laws of Manu 4:16

Crime and Punishment

Have no hatred for any being at all, for all who do thus shall come to me.
Bhagavad Gita 11:55

Non-violence is not passivity in any shape or form. It is the most active force in the world.
Mahatma Gandhi

War and Peace

An eye for an eye and we shall soon all be blind.
Mahatma Gandhi

Having regard to your duty, you should not hesitate, because for a warrior there is nothing greater than a just war. But if you do not fight in this just war, you will neglect your varna (duty), harm your reputation and commit the sin of omission.
Bhagavad Gita 2:31-32

Islam — Scriptural Quotes

The Natural World/Reverence for Life

There is not a beast on the earth but Allah is responsible for its sustenance. He knows its lair and its resting place.
Qur'an 11:8

Do not take life – which Allah has made sacred – except for a just cause.
Qur'an 17:33

If someone kills a sparrow for sport, the sparrow will cry out on the Day of Judgement, 'O Lord! That person killed me for nothing! He did not kill me for any useful purpose.'
Hadith

Body Matters

O you who believe, do not come to prayer with a befogged mind, but come when you can fully understand all that you are saying.
Qur'an 4:43

Do not harm yourself or others.
Hadith

Crime and Punishment

If the enemy inclines towards peace, then you should also incline towards peace and trust in Allah.
Qur'an 8:61

Goodness and evil cannot be equal. Repay evil with what is better, then the person who was your enemy will become your intimate friend.
Qur'an 41:34

The reward for an injury is an equal injury back, but if a person forgives instead, and is reconciled, that will earn reward from Allah.
Qur'an 42:40

As to the thief, male or female, cut off their hands: a punishment by way of an example.
Qur'an 3:41

War and Peace

The most excellent jihad [holy war] is to speak the truth in the face of a tyrannical ruler.
Hadith

Hate your enemy mildly; he may become your friend one day.
Hadith

Fight in the way of Allah with those who fight with you, but aggress not: God loves not the aggressors.
Qur'an 2:187

Judaism

Scriptural Quotes

The Natural World/Reverence for Life

A righteous man cares for the needs of his animal.
Proverbs 12:10

Be fruitful and increase in number, and fill the earth and subdue it. Rule over the fish of the sea and over the birds of the air and over every living creature that moves on the ground.
Genesis 1:28

Body Matters

Do not join those who drink too much wine or gorge themselves on meat.
Proverbs 23:20

Crime and Punishment

Anyone who strikes a man and kills him shall surely be put to death.
Exodus 21:12

Appoint judges and other officials in every town that the Lord your God gives you. These men are to judge the people impartially.
Deuteronomy 16:18

If your enemy is hungry give him food to eat. If he is thirsty give him water to drink.
Proverbs 25:21

War and Peace

He [God] will be judge between many peoples and will settle disputes for strong nations far and wide. They will beat their swords into ploughshares and their spears into pruning hooks; nation will not take up sword against nation nor will they train for war any more.
Micah 4:3

When you lay seige to a city ... do not destroy its trees by putting an axe to them because you can eat their fruit.
Deuteronomy 20:19

If a man has made a false accusation against his fellow-Israelite, he is to receive the punishment the accused man would have received. In this way you will get rid of evil.
Deuteronomy 19:18–19

Sikhism — Scriptural Quotes

The Natural World/Reverence for Life

Every creature is noble, none is low. God, the one potter, has made all things. God's light alone pervades creation.
Adi Granth 62

Body Matters

Wine takes away sense and leads people to madness, to the point where they cannot see wrong from right, to the point where they lose sight of God.
Adi Granth 554

Sikhs should not partake of alcohol, tobacco, drugs or other intoxicants.
Rehat Maryada: Discipline of the 'Word'

With God who knows all there can be no argument. He alone is Master, his decree absolute. Lords, kings and commanders of armies act to his command. We arrive in the world because God sends us into it. When God calls us back, we depart.
Adi Granth 1239

Crime and Punishment

He who associates with evil is destroyed. Being fed on poison his life goes to waste.
Adi Granth 1343

War and Peace

When all efforts to restore peace prove useless and no words avail, lawful is the flash of steel, it is right to draw the sword.
Guru Gobind Singh

O kind Father, loving Father, through thy mercy we have spent our day in peace and happiness; grant that we may, according to thy will, do what is right.
Prayer of Guru Gobind Singh

7 Nativity

Overview

A factor which affects every religion and which students need to be able to identify and take into account is the context of popular or secular tradition which builds up around it. Religion shapes people and their daily lives. Equally people can shape the circumstances in which religion is practised. For example, the celebration of marriage often combines religious rites with local secular traditions. Similarly, scripture is not immune to embellishment, particularly scripture which has a narrative or story-telling element.

Stories to do with an event celebrated at a major festival are regularly rehearsed, often in secular as well as religious ways. These are the stories we absorb at an early age, together with all their embellishments, and at subsequent retellings accept unquestioningly. *Nativity* is an activity that challenges students to look critically at the religious story which gets the most public attention in Britain each year, the Christian Nativity. Students have to unravel biblical accounts from popular additions and reflect on both the nature of scripture in telling stories and the reasons why scriptural accounts are sometimes embellished.

Objectives

By the end of this activity, students should be able to:

- accurately retell the Nativity story according to the Gospel accounts;
- explain how the original Nativity story has been embellished;
- reflect upon and evaluate the reasons why these embellishments have occurred.

Materials needed

Photocopiable
- *Nativity* sheet(s) (pp. 56–7) – 1 set for each of 5 groups
- *The King Spin* – (pp. 58–9) 5 copies, 1 for each of 4 student readers plus 1 for you as teacher

Other
- Large sheet of blank paper for a wall-frieze
- Assorted paper for 5 group illustrations
- Coloured pens and pencils
- Scissors
- Blu-Tack
- One or several versions of the Bible

Your role as teacher
- Organizer
- Discussion leader
- Reader

Classroom environment

Arrange furniture to allow students to work together in five groups on a practical, art-based activity. Clear and prepare one large wall-space for displaying finished work as a frieze, with space in front of it for the class to gather round.

Nativity

The activity step by step

1 Give a brief introduction to the five parts of the Nativity story: the annunciation; the journey from Nazareth and the birth; the shepherds; the wise men; the escape to Egypt.

2 Organize this opening task:
(i) Students work in five groups. Each group is given one of the parts of the Nativity story to illustrate.
(ii) Initially students brainstorm the task: the content they need to show and their approach. Then they collectively produce their group illustrations, using the large sheets of paper and drawing materials provided.
(iii) When groups have finished, they display their work in the form of a wall-frieze, putting up their illustrations in the correct sequence of the story.

3 Invite the whole class to gather round the frieze. Lead a discussion about what the students can see.

4 Organize this task:
The five groups reconvene and receive one set of *Nativity* sheets. They consider the relevance and validity of the material on the sheets to the Nativity story, noting any aspects or details which they think are inaccurate or unjustified.

5 With the whole class gathered round the frieze again, lead a discussion about any changes that should be made to the illustrations. Bring in issues which students identified when working on the *Nativity* sheets.

6 With three or four volunteer students (you need to decide whether you want to take up a role), read *The King Spin* sketch. Ask the class to point out further changes that should now be made to the frieze.

7 Read to the class the Bible passages (Matthew 1:18–2:23, Luke 1:26–56 and Luke 2) which contain the only evidence from Christian scriptures about the Nativity. Invite the class to make any concluding changes to the frieze.

Adapting the activity

For less-able students
At stage 3, provide Christmas cards with religious themes as well as the *Nativity* sheets. You may also want to consider whether *The King Spin* sketch is suitable or if it needs rehearsal before the lesson.

For more-able students
At stage 3, introduce copies of art works showing the Nativity (a postcard collection is published by National Gallery Publications Ltd, 5–6 Pall Mall East, London SW1Y 5BA; tel. 0171 839 8544). Also, invite students to consider whether or not fictitious additions to the biblical account of the Nativity help in communicating the significance of Jesus' birth.

Homework

Ask students to write a short piece on possible reasons for the biblical account of the Nativity having been changed so much.
Ask more-able students to focus their piece particularly on features to be found in artistic representations.

Changing the focus

Base the activity on the Easter story, divided into six sections: Palm Sunday and Jesus' entry into Jerusalem; Jesus' betrayal and arrest; the trials; the 'stations of the cross'; the crucifixion and Jesus' death; the resurrection.

When you need to tell or refer to the Easter story, select from these biblical passages: Matthew 21:1–11 and 26:1–28:20; Luke 19:28–44 and 22:1–24:12; Mark 11:1–11 and 14:12–16:20.

Nativity

The Virgin's name was Mary. And the angel came unto her.	Thou shalt conceive in thy womb, and bring forth a son, and shalt call his name Jesus.	Joseph, thou son of David, fear not to take unto thee Mary thy wife, for that which is conceived in her is of the Holy Spirit.
Pluck me one cherry, Joseph, for I am with child.	And it came to pass that there went out a decree from Caesar Augustus, that all the world should be taxed.	In the bleak mid-winter, frosty wind made moan.
And Joseph went up from Galilee, out of the city of Nazareth, into Judaea, unto the city of David, which is called Bethlehem.	Joseph was an old man, an old man was he.	And she brought forth her first born son ...
... there was sweet music at this child's birth ...	... and wrapped him in swaddling clothes, and laid him in a manger; because there was no room for them in the inn.	And there were in the same country shepherds abiding in the field ...
... all seated on the ground ...	... amid the winter's snow	... keeping watch over their flock by night.
The Angel of the Lord came upon them ...	... with wings as drifted snow and eyes as flames.	There was with the Angel a multitude of the heavenly host praising God.

Nativity

The shepherds said one to another, let us go now to Bethlehem ...	... torches, torches, run with torches all the way to Bethlehem.	And they came in haste ...
... a shepherd-boy piping on the way ...	... and found Mary, and Joseph, and the babe lying in a manger.	Cold on his cradle the dewdrops are shining.
May we stroke the creatures there, ox, ass or sheep?	Cheese from the dairy, bring they for Mary.	The cattle are lowing, the baby awakes.
Little Jesus, sweetly sleep, do not stir, we will lend a coat of fur.	And the shepherds returned, glorifying and praising God for all the things that they had heard and seen.	... Three ships come sailing in.
There came wise men from the east to Jerusalem, saying ...	We three kings of Orient are.	When King Herod heard these things he was troubled.
Bring me word again that I may come and worship him.	For we have seen his star in the east.	They presented unto him gifts, gold, frankincense, and myrrh.

The King Spin

A courtroom: four characters are present.

Lawyer 1 Let me summarize the plaintiff's case, your honour. My client, Mr King, is claiming substantial compensation for loss of royalties due to him from the producers and distributors of items such as celebratory cards, calendars, school plays, television comedy specials, phonograph records, interactive CDs, seasonal menswear items and a range of novelty goods commemorating the birth of a certain Jesus Christ, in the events surrounding which he claims to have had a not inconsiderable involvement.

Mr King I'm the one with the beard and the crown. There were three of us – all kings.

Lawyer 1 Quite.

Lawyer 2 [rising] Mr King, let me get straight to the point. I put it to you plainly that your claim is based on fiction.

Mr King Look, it's all in the Bible.

Lawyer 2 What is?

Mr King The story people tell about the birth of Jesus.

Lawyer 2 Are you quite sure about that, Mr King? Then please be so kind as to tell us where exactly.

Mr King The Gospels, mate.

Lawyer 2 In the Gospels. So the fact that Mark and John – two of the four Gospel writers, if I remember correctly – don't mention the birth of Jesus at all doesn't bother you?

Mr King Well, you know how it is. Slip of the pen.

Lawyer 2 Or perhaps they had no information.

Lawyer 1 Your honour, my client is over two thousand years old. He rode on a camel following a star. There are pictures of him all over people's mantlepieces at Christmas. Children still sing songs about him and his two kingly colleagues. What more conclusive evidence can there be?

Mr King And the shepherds. Don't forget the shepherds.

Lawyer 2 Ah, yes. All that charming rustic stuff. Tell us, Mr King, where was the baby Jesus born, as far as you know?

Mr King In a stable.

Lawyer 2 Ah, in a stable. So there must surely have been a few animals about. What were they, Mr King?

Mr King Let's see. An ox, and an ass ...

Lawyer 2 I see, but no chickens or sheep. A lot of chickens get into stables, you know.

Mr King Well, there might have been a few chickens. Yes, now I come to think of it, there were some chickens – and a couple of geese, maybe a duck.

Lawyer 2	So, let's get this clear. You're telling this court that in the stable where you visited the baby Jesus there was one ox, one ass, an unspecified number of chickens, two geese and in all probability a duck. What about goats? Any recollection of those?
Lawyer 1	[to the Judge] Your honour, is this line of questioning getting us anywhere?
Judge	[to Lawyer 2] Counsel?
Lawyer 2	Yes, your honour. It is my contention that there was no stable. According to the Bible, after Jesus was born he was placed in a manger, but that's all we know. The manger could have been anywhere.
Mr King	Come on, it was snowing when Jesus was born. He had to be born in some kind of shelter ...
Lawyer 2	Snowing? Is snow mentioned in the Gospel accounts, Mr King? Luke says that sheep were still being grazed in the fields. Normally they're brought in at the slightest hint of snow. It may even have been warm at the time – warm enough for Jesus to have been born quite comfortably in the open, wouldn't you say, Mr King?
Lawyer 1	Your honour, I object ...
Judge	Hypothetical question, counsel.
Lawyer 2	Exactly my point, your honour. When evidence is as patchy as this, people start filling in the gaps. They hypothesize. Then they forget which parts are made up, and the whole story gets embroidered. And that brings me to this question for Mr King: do you or any of your acquaintances consider that you might in any way be a magus?
Mr King	[jumping to his feet] Come outside and say that!
Lawyer 2	Obviously not, Mr King. You may be interested to know that Matthew is the only Gospel writer to refer to the people who followed a star from the East, as you claim to have done, and he calls them magi – wise men – not kings.
Mr King	Yeah, yeah, now I come to think of it people did call us magi. That's right. 'Look at those three magi!' they said when we arrived at the stable.
Lawyer 2	'Three magi', Mr King? Where do you get the 'three' from? We know of the three types of gift which the magi brought to Jesus – gold, frankincense and myrrh – but no one has the slightest idea how many magi there were. There must have been more than one, of course. And you also mentioned arriving at the stable, presumably to visit Jesus after your long journey to Bethlehem. But didn't you see Jesus in a house, Mr King?
Mr King	House? What, with tables and chairs and stuff? Don't be daft. You've seen the pictures – animals, straw, lamplight ...
Lawyer 2	And I've read the evidence. Only Matthew writes about this, and 'house' is clearly, and solely, what he says.
Judge	Look here, Mr King, old chap, sorry to be a party pooper, but I'm afraid your case seems to be crumbling like a supermarket Christmas cake. Let's face it, you just weren't there, were you?
Mr King	Nor was Santa Claus.
Judge	Exactly my point. Mr Balthazar King, your case is dismissed.

8 Pilgrimage

Overview

One of the challenges of looking at pilgrimage in the classroom is that 'looking' – using evidence on video, for instance – can often be the main learning activity. Surrounding the topic is an air of remoteness, not helped by seeing places and rituals as an outside observer. Most pilgrimage sites are in far-off places. The importance and significance of being a pilgrim is tied up with religious identity and individual spirituality, easy to acknowledge but much more difficult to appreciate. To pupils whose backgrounds give them no direct insights, pilgrimage can sometimes seem like a journey leading away from the world as they know it.

Distance, and overcoming it, is part of the challenge and sacrifice of undertaking a pilgrimage. For participants, one of the rewards of successfully completing a pilgrimage is the unique experience of having been to a place or places of profound religious and therefore personal significance – whatever the location. In *Pilgrimage,* understanding the significance of being at a pilgrimage site, either as a member of a faith community or with some other specific purpose, is the starting-point and focus for pupils' research and evaluation.

The setting is Israel. The pilgrimage sites are Masada, Jerusalem and Bethlehem. The faith traditions are Judaism, Islam and Christianity.

Objectives

By the end of this activity, students should be able to:

- explain why certain places have become pilgrimage sites;
- describe and explain the rituals associated with specific pilgrimage sites;
- reflect on the thoughts and emotions that a visit to these sites may evoke in people of different backgrounds.

Materials needed

Photocopiable
- *'You are ...' cards* (p. 62) – one set for each of five groups; there are eight different cards, allowing some scope for selection

Other
- 15 large sheets of paper
- Reference books, selected to include material on Jerusalem, Bethlehem and Masada as pilgrimage sites

Your role as teacher

- Organizer

Classroom environment

Arrange furniture to allow five groups of about six students each to undertake research and written work and to move round the room to view the work of other groups.

Pilgrimage

The activity step by step

1 Divide the class into five groups of about six students each. Give each group one set of *'You are ...' cards*.

2 Organize this opening task:
(i) Working individually, students each take one *'You are ...'* card from the set given to their group. Their card identifies who they are, where they are, and a particular moment.
(ii) Students use the reference books and other information sources to research the pilgrimage site that their card identifies. As they do this, they take into account issues to do with the personal viewpoint they have been given – issues such as why that person is there and what they expect to gain from their visit. Students make relevant notes as they work.

3 Give each group three large sheets of paper, then organize this task:
(i) Working in their groups, students write the heading 'Judaism' on one sheet, 'Islam' on another and 'Christianity' on the third.
(ii) On the appropriate sheet, students in turn write from the personal perspective they have been given the thoughts they feel might come to mind at the moment described in their *'You are ...'* card.
(iii) When this has been done, students circulate and read all the sheets from all the groups.

4 Organize this final task:
Working individually, students write from a Jewish, Muslim or Christian perspective, as relevant, a reflective piece about Masada, Jerusalem or Bethlehem, incorporating information about any rituals that take place there as well as reflections from other students that have impressed them.

Adapting the activity

For less-able students
At stage 3, help them with their reflective work by (a) providing additional resource material relevant to each pilgrimage site and (b) asking structured questions to guide the reflection process (for example, 'What did you feel like when the people started acting in the street on the Via Dolorosa?' or 'What prayer might you write on your piece of paper at the Western Wall?').

For more-able students
At stage 1, organize more-able students into a group to work together. At stage 3, when they have finished work based on their *'You are ...' cards*, ask the students to devise *'You are ...'* scenarios of their own for the pilgrimage sites and present them to the rest of the group.

Homework

Ask students to write a paragraph describing a place which is special to them personally and explaining why they like to go there.

Changing the focus

Choose other pilgrimages, such as Hajj, or other pilgrimage sites, such as Amritsar, and create appropriate *'You are ...'* cards for them. Remember that non-Muslims are not allowed to visit the holy places associated with Hajj.

'You are...' cards

- You are a 13-year-old Jewish boy.
- You have just had your Bar Mitzvah at the Western Wall.
- You have just placed your prayer in the Western Wall.

- You are a 65-year-old holocaust survivor.
- You are at Yad Vashem.
- You have just read the name of your concentration camp in the Hall of Remembrance.

- You are a tourist.
- You are standing on the barren top of Masada.
- Your tour guide has just told you the story of the siege.

- You are 11 and on a school trip.
- You have just visited the Church of the Nativity.
- You are looking for a souvenir to take home to Mum.

- You are a tourist visiting Jerusalem in the spring.
- You are standing in the Via Dolorosa.
- You are swamped by the crowds of people acting out the events of Good Friday when Simon of Cyrene took the cross from Jesus.

- You are a 40-year-old Christian.
- You are with a group of fellow Christians in the Garden of Gethsemane at sunset.
- You have just listened to a reading of the biblical passage on Jesus' vigil in the Garden (Mark 14: 32-42).

- You are a Hajji (a person who has completed the Muslim pilgrimage).
- You are standing on the Mount of Olives, looking out over the old city of Jerusalem.
- You suddenly see sunlight reflected vividly off a golden dome in the middle of the city.

- You are a 20-year-old Muslim.
- You have just walked through one of eight gateways that open into the courtyard that surrounds a very special octagonal mosque.
- You know that with a few more steps you could be standing on Mount Mariah, Ibrahim's place of sacrifice.

9 Moving Pictures

Overview

Some people state their opinions with such confidence that they make the process of arriving at an opinion seem deceptively simple. *Moving Pictures* is an activity that allows students to begin to understand more about the complex balance of factors which comes into play when people form and put forward an opinion. In particular, it places students in the position of experiencing, identifying and considering factors to do with emotional reactions and attitudes.

Issues in RE can have a significant emotional dimension, which is why the phrase 'I feel strongly about ...' is so often expressed or implied when students discuss their views in RE. The difficulty here is that whilst emotion can animate students' thinking in RE and lead to some genuine insights, especially where spirituality is concerned, the strong reactions and attitudes which are often stirred up by socially provocative issues can make it difficult for students to accept the validity of viewpoints or dimensions beyond those with which they have emotionally identified.

Moving Pictures is principally a non-verbal activity that requires students to indicate a reaction or attitude towards issues which unfold in a series of human-rights scenarios. At each successive stage, the focus changes sufficiently to challenge students' previous reactions or attitudes. By demonstrating emotional reactions and attitudes at work, *Moving Pictures* is able to help students recognize more skilfully not only the parts of their own thinking which are emotionally driven but any attitudes in the evidence they are handling which are likely to have been influenced by a strong emotional reaction.

Objectives

By the end of this activity, students should be able to reflect on their attitudes and reactions to a variety of human-rights issues.

Materials needed

Photocopiable
- Tableaux cards (p. 65) – 1 set for you to use as organizer

Other
- Signs for tableaux A, C and D

Your role as teacher

- Organizer
- Discussion leader

Classroom environment

Clear an open space large enough for a 'stage' area and a standing audience, or arrange to use a drama studio.

Moving Pictures

The activity step by step

1 Introduce the tableau activity:
(i) Students will be asked to respond to ideas without using words. During this activity, four 'human sculptures' or tableaux will be created. Each will involve a different group of students. Everyone will have an opportunity to take part in a tableau.
(ii) The tableau part of the activity will take place in silence. When students are not directly participating, they should observe and not talk.

2 Explain what will happen:
(i) As the teacher, you are the only participant allowed to talk whilst the tableaux are in progress. You will be allocating roles and setting up and modifying situations.
(ii) Students taking part in the tableaux should adopt a pose that reflects their attitude to what they see and hear.

3 Organize the tableaux:
(i) Take each tableau in turn and allocate the roles specified on the card. Ask the participants to adopt their poses. After a short time, change the sign placed beside the actor(s) and ask the other participants to change their poses if they wish to.
(ii) Allow time for discussion, which should take place after each tableau. Base the discussion on the reactions of the rest of the class and draw out the variety of attitudes portrayed and the changes in attitude that occurred.

Adapting the activity

For less-able students
Suggest key words which might help students involved in the tableau adopt their pose: e.g. fear, revulsion, pity, anger, sadness, power.

For more-able students
After they have worked through the first tableau, give the students themes based on human-rights issues and allow them to develop their own frameworks for tableaux.

Homework

Ask the students to watch a national television news bulletin then choose a story they have seen which has a human-rights angle and write a reflective piece based on it. The piece should record the students' attitudes and reactions towards the issue and the people concerned.

Changing the focus

With appropriate preparation, tableaux can be developed to explore dimensions within a single human-rights issue, such as racism or freedom of speech.

Tableaux cards

A Poverty

1 actor
5 passers-by

Put these signs in turn on the actor:

Beggar
Junkie
Homeless
Terminally ill

Actor poses as beggar in doorway. Passers-by take up poses to indicate their attitude towards the beggar.

After each change of sign, passers-by change their pose if the new information alters their attitudes.

B Aggression

1 actor
6 youths (any combination of girls and boys)

Actor poses as someone waiting alone in a public place. The youths surround the actor in an aggressive manner and adopt a pose.

C Captivity

1 actor
4 army officers

Put these signs in turn on the actor:

Captive
Hostage
Auschwitz internee
Child molester

Actor poses as a captive. The officers adopt a pose in relation to the captive.

After each change of sign, officers change their pose if the new information alters their attitudes.

D Love

2 actors
Rest of the class

Put these signs in turn on the couple:

John/Mary
brother/sister
William/Ben
Father George Dunn/Mrs Dawson
Ashed Hanson/Kelly Holmes
(or similar team-mates)

Actors embrace and hold the pose. Rest of the class adopt a pose in relation to the actors.

After each change of sign, class change their pose if the new information alters their attitudes.

10 Afterthoughts

Overview

Wherever possible, good RE draws on and refers to the personal experience of students, and this link helps them to learn from as well as about religion. But some topics – like death and the afterlife – are well outside the terms of reference of most students, and those few who do have experience may not want to acknowledge it or share it with others, especially in an exposed forum like an RE lesson. Sensitive to the issues that surround 'difficult' topics like this, some RE teachers restrict their approach so that open-ended activity such as discussion is avoided. However, the result can be superficial or remote – and predictably so. An important topic like death and the afterlife, which lies at the heart of so much religious thinking and practice and provides such important insights into the character of each of the major world faiths, deserves better treatment.

Afterthoughts is constructed around a type of evidence not used elsewhere in this book: the personal views and experience of religious believers. Material of this sort brings a special quality to RE and introduces into the classroom an authenticity similar to that offered by the personal experience of students. As an evidence base it is capable of animating the meaning of religious belief and practice in ways which ordinary textbook descriptions are simply not equipped to do – by providing, instead of detailed analysis, moments of simple insight. This makes it especially suited to taking personal experience in the RE classroom into areas which would otherwise be too inaccessible or sensitive to be tackled in this way.

Objectives

By the end of this activity students should be able to reflect upon concepts of the afterlife and evaluate their own attitudes and feelings concerning death.

Materials needed

Photocopiable
- *Death card* (p.68) – 1 per student
- *Statements* (pp.69–72) – 1 set per pair

Other
- Small container
- Five poster-sized sheets of paper, each with one letter from DEATH written at the top
- Five marker-pens
- Three felt-tip pens, each a different colour
- Blu-Tack or sticky tape

Your role as teacher
- Organizer
- Discussion leader

Classroom environment

Arrange chairs in a horseshoe, allowing an open view of the board. No tables are required. Students can work individually, in pairs and as a group in this formation. Writing takes place on laps or on the floor.

Afterthoughts

The activity step by step

1 Organize this opening task:
Each student is given a 'death' card (see p.68). Working individually, they write a word or short phrase beginning with each of the initial letters (D, E, A, T, H) to express their thoughts and feelings about death. They then put their completed card in the small container.

2 Select five students to be scribes and give each of them one of the poster-sized sheets headed with a letter from DEATH. Then organize this whole-class task:
(i) The rest of the students in turn draw one completed death card each from the container. One by one round the class they read out the words or phrases on their card written against the letter D; the scribe in charge of the D poster writes these down. The process is repeated with the other four letters.
(ii) When the task has been completed, the five poster sheets are put on display so that students can see the range of thoughts and ideas.

3 Select three further students as scribes and give each a coloured felt-tip pen. Explain to the scribes and the class that each pen is a different colour. The colours correspond to the three categories into which the words and phrases on each poster are about to be sorted. For instance, blue is for 'concept'; red is for 'feelings'; green is 'other'.
Taking each poster in turn, read words and phrases to the class. The students have to discuss and agree a category for each word or phrase, and the scribe with the relevant pen then underlines it.

4 Look again at the words and phrases. Ask the class to identify all those which can be described as either positive or negative. One of the scribes marks the class verdict ('+ve' or '-ve') against each relevant word or phrase.

5 Lead a general discussion about the words and the balance between positive and negative in the feelings and concepts they convey.

6 Organize this task:
Students work in pairs. Each pair is given a *Statements* sheet. They consider the statements on the sheet and write '+ve' or '-ve' against any for which this is a valid judgement.

7 Ask the pairs to tell the rest of the class what they found. With the whole class, reflect on the attitudes to death and the afterlife expressed in the statements. Have any students encountered ideas here which prompt them to re-evaluate their own attitudes towards death and the afterlife?

Adapting the activity

For less-able students
Provide *Death cards* with some words and phrases already in place. For example:
    D – distress, devil
    E – eternity, everlasting
    A – ashes, anger
    T – tomb, terror
    H – hearse, Heaven

For more-able students
Ask students to write at least six words or phrases for each letter on their *Death cards*.

Homework

Ask students to write a short reflective piece in which they consider their own ideas about death and the afterlife in the light of the religious ideas they have explored.

Death cards

D
E
A
T
H

Statements

We are constantly identified with our bodies. We think, 'This is me', or 'I am my body, I am these thoughts, I am these feelings, I am these desires, I am this wealth, these beautiful possessions that I have, this personality.'

That's where we go wrong. Through our ignorance we go chasing after shadows, dwelling in delusion, unable to face the storms that life brings us. We're not able to stand like those oak trees along the boundary of the meadow – that stay all winter long and weather every storm that comes their way. In October, they drop their leaves so gracefully. And in the spring they bloom again.

For us too there are comings and goings, the births and deaths, the seasons of our lives. When we are ready, and even if we are not ready, we will die. Even if we never fall sick a day in our lives, we still die. That's what bodies are supposed to do.

Sister Medhanandi, Theravada Buddhist nun

In Orthodoxy, we see less division than some people do between the living and the dead. We remember that Jesus said, 'God is not a God of the dead, but of the living: for all live unto him.' We don't see death as such a final, decisive moment. This means we feel able to talk to those who have gone ahead of us into eternity and who now live there. We expect to have a personal relationship with the saints.

In the Orthodox church, when somebody dies they are brought in an open coffin into the church, where they lie in a corner. If they're there on a Sunday, the service goes on around them. This is because they're still included in the congregation. People can and do go up and stand and pray with the dead person. We conduct our funerals standing round an open coffin and at the end of it come up to give the dead person a last kiss.

Gillian, member of the Eastern Orthodox Church

Statements

Quakers have meetings for special purposes, and one which I find particularly powerful and moving is our memorial meeting. It's a Quaker funeral. Obviously, people who come to a Quaker funeral bring with them a complex mass of emotions. But in amongst all that is a strong focus on thanksgiving for the person's life. The type of contribution I find most moving is when people remember the person's life and all the good things about it.

Perry, practising Quaker

Death seems to me such a wonderful opportunity if only we'd use it. I don't say I enjoy taking funerals, but I like the funerals of people who've died well. They've gone through all the stages of feeling anger and rejection and hope and fear. They've planned things. Finally at the end there's an incredible acceptance. That's a good death.

People do actually die as they live. If they've been selfish all their lives, they go on being selfish when they're dying. They won't talk to anybody about it or help their families make plans for life without them. They leave their friends and relatives shattered.

Father Neville, Anglican Christian

Rashid started talking to the men in the hall. He spoke about Islam and about what would happen to them when they died, because death is definite – it's guaranteed for everyone. Once he started talking about death and people having to answer for their actions, the snooker stopped. Everyone froze. Their attention was focused on this one guy. About thirty men – they were Muslims – left their snooker and came over to listen to him.

Ifzal, practising Muslim

When I think of the Day of Judgement, I think of myself standing in front of Allah with everybody else. All human beings are there. Each of us goes in front of Allah in turn and answers for our actions. When you are there in front of Allah, every part of your body speaks. If a thief goes in front of Allah, his hands speak for what he's stolen and his feet speak for taking him to the places where he stole things. You account for your actions, then God decides whether to place you in Heaven or in Hell.

Andleeb, practising Muslim

Statements

The Jewish way of death and mourning provides specific ritual. It assumes that upon death, the soul departs the body for 'the world to come' – a concept prayed for throughout life and generally interpreted by individuals themselves. The theory of heaven and hell do not exist but during one's lifetime, one aspires to perform a sufficiency of good deeds (both formal and informal) to qualify one's soul/spirit for a place in 'the world to come'.

To assure peace and comfort to the soul of the departed, specific prayers, psalms and memorial readings are recited at the funeral and daily for 11 months thereafter. During the first seven days, which period is known as 'shiva', the Hebrew word for seven, it is customary to visit the mourners, bringing food and comfort. This period of 'shiva' forms a cushioning between the sorrowful event and the return to normal life and work.

To many, the 'world to come' is also expressed as eternal life. When the approach of death is recognized, there is a prayer of confession and forgiveness to be said. I quote below some extracts from prayers which convey the thoughts and atmosphere surrounding death:

'As for man, his days are as grass; as the flower of the field, so he flourisheth. For the wind passeth over it, and it is gone; and the place thereof shall know it no more. But the loving kindness of the Lord is from everlasting to everlasting upon them that fear him.'

'In the way of righteousness is life; and in the pathway thereof there is no death. And the dust returneth to the earth as it was, but the spirit returneth unto God, who gave it.'

'The Lord gave, and the Lord hath taken away; blessed be the name of the Lord. And he, being merciful, forgiveth iniquity and destroyeth not.'

People who have been present at an interment wash their hands in a symbolic gesture and say, 'He maketh death to vanish in life eternal; and the Lord God wipeth away tears from off all faces; and the reproach of his people shall be taken away from all the earth: for the Lord hath spoken it.'

Edna, Orthodox Jew

Statements

Death in Judaism entails immediate and dignified respect for the dead since they can no longer speak on their own behalf.

This respect also means that someone is always with the body during the period that the soul ascends to its place; Heaven being equated with the Garden of Eden, Paradise, or the world to come.

Burial takes place within the shortest possible time after death.

Visiting in order to comfort and care for the bereaved or just with one's presence, is imperative in the week after the funeral. People would feel this as an urgent and sincere duty.

The mourning by the bereaved family is observed for up to 11 months following the funeral.

Louis, Orthodox Jew

According to Sikhism, the individual soul has arrived at the human form after going through innumerable cycles of birth and death. Now at last it may try for the final spiritual evolution, so that it may be freed from further transmigration and return to its source.

Death has been interpreted in different ways. According to the general concept death is the extinction of the body and the sense organs.

To conquer death is to merit salvation. Death has a terror for ordinary mortals. They are afraid because they have not made any progress on the spiritual plane. They feel worried for their sins and fear punishment for their misdeeds.

A 'true' devotee welcomes death as a friend and as a benefactor because he or she looks forward to a union with the Supreme Being. They know that it is through the gate of physical death that they will be able to embrace their beloved Lord. Death is nothing but a gateway to Divinity and Eternity.

Raminder, practising Sikh